Praise for *100 Tough Questions for Catholics*

"Catholics have never been afraid to ask questions, and this book is chock-full of some of the toughest ones out there. And they are tough precisely because they are on matters that are so important. From science and medicine, to sexuality, to proper worship, even to life on other planets — readers of this book will be exposed to an incredibly wide range of topics. The Catholic in your life who has questions about the Church will certainly appreciate this book!"

— *Timothy Cardinal Dolan*, Archbishop of New York

"In clear, logical, orderly language, David Bonagura presents answers to foundational questions troubling many people, young and old, at present. His is a mission of hope, sometimes reminiscent of the solidity of the old *Baltimore Catechism*, which will lead many readers into the ways of the Faith and on to the inexhaustible riches of Catholic Tradition. This is a book to give to anyone who is seeking and needs help to find or for anyone who needs a quick refresher on the basics of Catholic belief."

— *Robert Royal*, President, Faith & Reason Institute

"Bonagura adeptly blends apologetic vigor with catechetical acumen in this exceptional book. His approach is pithy and precise, covering much ground with accessible writing and orthodox wisdom."

— *Carl E. Olson*, Editor, *Catholic World Report*

"David Bonagura has given us a very welcome remedy to the prevalent religious ignorance and errors of our times. His readable, concise, and well-argued answers to tough questions will instruct and inspire Catholics, and anyone else seeking guidance, to see God and the Catholic Faith in a new light. A delightful read."

— *Fr. Gerald E. Murray*, Pastor, St. Joseph's Church, New York; member, EWTN's *The Papal Posse!*

100 TOUGH QUESTIONS
FOR CATHOLICS

David G. Bonagura, Jr.

100
TOUGH
QUESTIONS
FOR
CATHOLICS

COMMON OBSTACLES
TO FAITH TODAY

SOPHIA INSTITUTE PRESS
Manchester, New Hampshire

Cover by LUCAS Art & Design, Jenison, MI

Cover image: Church, Stained glass, Cathedral image by TAMA66 (Pixabay 3599448)

NIHIL OBSTAT
Rev. Walter Kedjierski, Ph.D.
Censor Deputatus

IMPRIMATUR
Most Rev. John O. Barres, S.T.D., J.C.L., Bishop of Rockville Centre
October 22, 2024

Sophia Institute Press
Box 5284, Manchester, NH 03108
1-800-888-9344
www.SophiaInstitute.com

Sophia Institute Press is a registered trademark of Sophia Institute.

paperback ISBN 979-8-88911-352-2

ebook ISBN 979-8-88911-353-9

Library of Congress Control Number: 2024951836

First printing

CONTENTS

Contents

Contents

100 TOUGH QUESTIONS
FOR CATHOLICS

INTRODUCTION
CLEARING OBSTACLES TO FAITH

†

Studies show that the chief reason young people leave the Catholic Church is because their questions about their Faith are not answered. They have questions about every aspect of the supernatural life: "Is God real or not?" "If God is real, why is there evil in the world?" "Is there really an afterlife?" "Why don't my prayers always get answered?" "Why is sex such a big deal to religions and churches?" They struggle not because they cannot find answers to abstract, intellectual questions but because these questions strike their hearts as much as their heads. They seek a sure path on which to walk the journey of life, and they expect Catholicism to provide it. So, when these sincere questions go unanswered, they grow disillusioned. If religion cannot answer their deepest questions, they figure, then it is not worth their time. They slowly withdraw from the Church until they stop showing up at all.

A further challenge exists today both for young people and for Catholics of all ages: Popular culture, which is inherently secular and hostile to religion, generates the framework for so many of these questions. Religion is made to seem retrograde, foreign to a modern world teeming with scientific power, and opposed to personal fulfillment. Many of the most frequent questions people have today put Catholicism on trial, as if it has committed some sort of crime and is guilty until proven innocent.

Adding to this problem, God is almost never mentioned in public places these days — public schools and universities, workplaces and offices, athletic fields and gymnasiums, bars and clubs — except when His name is taken in vain. Whenever anything related to religion is mentioned on the news or in media, it is typically negative: crimes committed by clergy, vandalism of church properties, disputes about religious teachings.

Put simply, multiple obstacles stand in the way of Catholics developing and living out an authentic life of faith within the loving embrace of the Church.

This book aims to clear away those obstacles by answering one hundred of the most repeated, pressing, and hot-button questions that Catholics have about their Faith today. They are authentic questions, submitted anonymously by young Catholics in New York City. No controversial issue is left unaddressed: God and evolution, Jesus Christ and salvation, the Bible and science, Catholicism and other religions, sex and gender.

My answers get right to the point. Often, these answers require a broader context, as the issues raised are not isolated one-offs but are outgrowths from a single tree. To understand the leaves, so to speak, it is necessary to see them as part of a branch that grows from a wider trunk. The trunk stands firm because it possesses firm roots that dig deeply into the soil. The Church calls the trunk the *deposit of faith*, which is the revelation of God to human beings in the Old and New Testaments and taught by the Catholic Church. Once this foundational context is understood, answers to particular questions follow quickly. I have arranged the questions by theme so that they better reflect the image of Catholicism as a single tree with many branches and leaves. Because of this close connection of the Church's teachings, many of the answers to the following questions refer to other ones in different chapters. The questions are numbered consecutively to facilitate cross-referencing.

By removing the obstacles to faith that these questions pose, Catholics can then embrace their Faith and live it to the full. Faith expresses a personal relationship with the living God who is Father, Son, and Holy Spirit. By Baptism, each Catholic becomes an adopted child of God and a brother or sister of Jesus Christ. In other words, being Catholic is about entering into the love of God. God loves each one of us more than we can comprehend, and He desperately desires us to love Him in return.

It is necessary, then, to clear these obstacles to faith as quickly as possible so that fallen-away Catholics can come home, so that those raised outside the Church can build their houses on the rock of Jesus Christ, and so that believers beleaguered by a hostile secular world can experience the love that God has for them and share that love with others.

CHAPTER 1

GOD, DIVINE REVELATION, HUMAN BEINGS, AND FREE WILL

†

1. *WHAT IS GOD?*

God transcends the limits of the human mind and of human speech. Words fail us whenever we attempt to describe Him. Acknowledging this fact, we can say that God is not merely the Supreme Being, but Being existing in Himself: pure power, pure action, pure existence. In other words, it has been said that we can understand God not as a noun, but as a verb.

God is complete in Himself; He lacks nothing and does not need anything. He is perfect goodness. He has always existed — there is no beginning, middle, or end in God; rather, He is the author of time. All things that exist — the universe, the galaxies, the planets, life on earth — are products of His creative thought, and they all work according to a discernible order that God has designed. God creates because He desires to share His goodness with His creatures. Creation and its order are evidence of God's existence.

Over time God revealed Himself directly to human beings in order to establish a personal relationship with us. The Church has received God's revelation and handed it on through her teachings, sacraments, and the Bible itself, which teaches that God is love and that His love pours out from the very essence of His being, for the one God is a Trinity of Persons — Father, Son, and Holy Spirit — who mutually love one another.

When we say that God is love, we mean that the Father, Son, and Holy Spirit perpetually will the good for one another without beginning or end. The power of this love exceeds human comprehension, but we can see its result in the fact that the world and human beings exist. Love is effusive — it cannot be contained. God's love is so powerful that, as it overflows, it creates everything that exists and sustains it in being.

God is neither male nor female. He is pure spirit; He does not have a body or any physical parts. It is proper to speak of God with masculine pronouns because, through Jesus, God reveals Himself to us as "Father," the generator of all creation and of all life.

It is helpful to consider what God is not. He is not, as many prominent atheist writers have alleged, a kind of supercomputer whose complex algorithms dictate every aspect of creation. Nor is He an old man in the sky angrily observing the earth and waiting to punish those who transgress His laws. No. As pure action, pure love, pure power, God is Being in perpetual action, directing all things by virtue of His creative and loving will.

2. HOW DO WE KNOW FOR SURE THAT GOD EXISTS?

The existence of God cannot be proven like a math problem, yet there is tremendous rational and experiential evidence that demonstrates that believing in God is most reasonable.

Two kinds of rational evidence, discovered by the power of logical human thought reflecting on the world, testify to God's existence. The first is the *argument of contingency*: Everything we have experienced in the world depends on something else before it; nothing in the world has caused its own existence. In other words, something does not come from nothing. For anything to exist, then, something outside of the chain of existence must have put things in motion. For example, for a mechanical assembly line to work, something outside of it has to turn it on. Analogously, that something outside of the entire order of existence that puts the world into motion we call God.

The second piece of rational evidence is the *design or order of the universe*: Every aspect of it, from the motion of the planets to the inner workings of the human body, is intricately designed and functions according to an extremely precise order. The slightest changes in gravity, the composition of the atmosphere, or the speed of the earth's rotation would cause life to cease to exist. In a similar way, we know that a computer is intricately designed by its manufacturer — it did not cause itself. Further, all its component parts had to be arranged into the right places for it to function properly. The parts do not find order themselves; someone outside of the machine had to harmonize them. The universe and the world could not exist with the grand order that they possess without some mind to design them and set them in motion; we call the designer God.

God can also be known through our *experiences*, which are often more convincing reasons to believe in Him than the rational ones. Through our experiences we can see God with our heart rather than our eyes. When events work out too well to be a mere coincidence, when we encounter someone whom we had thought about earlier in the day, when we feel a sudden calm during a tense situation, when we are startled into action by a stinging reprimand, we can feel the presence of God calling us to Himself by His orchestration of these events. In the eyes of God, there are no coincidences.

Finally, we experience God in our *consciences*, where our innate sense of right and wrong, good and evil, point to a Divine Lawgiver who is the source of all good and the judge of all action. Conscience is often understood as a "voice" that speaks to us from within. The voice calling us to do good is God Himself.

This evidence together provides ample reason to believe that God exists — both our minds and our hearts point us to this reality. Moreover, God's existence cannot be disproven. The two preferred arguments of atheists against God's existence, that evil exists in the world and that some prayers seemingly go unanswered (Q20, 77-78), not only say nothing about God but also fail to answer the rational and experiential arguments mentioned here. The argument for God's existence is much stronger than the argument against it.

Belief in God cannot be compelled. Each person has to weigh the evidence for himself and then make the conscious decision to entrust himself to God. We call the act of entrusting ourselves to God *faith*. When we make that act of faith, that act of giving ourselves to God, He always receives us with His unbounded love.

3. *WHY SHOULD I BELIEVE GOD LOVES ME?*

God loves you immensely, more than you can possibly imagine. God purposefully created you and willed you into existence with a specific plan for you: that you live forever with Him. What God said to the prophet Jeremiah He says to you: "Before I formed you in the womb I knew you, and before you were born I consecrated you" (Jer. 1:5).

God loves you unconditionally. Even on your worst day, even after you have committed terrible sins, even after the world has given up on you because your looks or abilities do not meet its standards, God loves you. You may feel horrible because you did not make a team or get into a school, lost your job or your significant other, hurt someone dear to you, or did something gravely wrong. Yet God still loves you and will never withdraw from you. He is your reason for living when everything else seems like a lost cause. He remains by your side in support when everyone else has abandoned you.

Too many people make a fateful mistake: they assume that God does not love them because of what they have done. As a result, they put up barriers to God: they stop going to church and refuse to hear about Him. Living this way is wrong. Jesus made it abundantly clear in His ministry that His very mission is to rescue sinners from the prisons in which they have trapped themselves: "I have not come to call the righteous, but sinners to repentance" (Luke 5:32).

St. Alphonsus Ligouri put it best: "God loves you more than you love yourself; what do you fear?" God's love is irrevocable, but He will never force us to accept it. It is incumbent upon you to overcome your fears about God or about the state of your life and then reach out to Him and receive His love. If you do, you will not be disappointed.

4. IF GOD IS OMNIPOTENT, WHY DOES HE ALLOW NATURAL DISASTERS?

To consider this question, we need a measure of humility: we do not have a rational answer for why God allows natural disasters to claim lives and destroy livelihoods. We simply do not know. In the Bible, God teaches Job — who is wondering what God is doing to him after he suffers the loss of his property, the death of his children, and physical maladies as a result of Satan's machinations — that we human beings are part of the film, so to speak; we do not have access to the director's notes for how the film's action will play itself out. God challenges Job with a series of rhetorical questions:

> Where were you when I laid the foundation of the
> earth? Tell me, if you have understanding. Who deter-
> mined its measurements — surely you know!... Has
> the rain a father, or who has begotten the drops of
> dew? From whose womb did the ice come forth, and
> who has given birth to the hoarfrost of heaven?...
> Who can number the clouds by wisdom?... Do you
> give the horse his might?... Is it by your wisdom that
> the hawk soars? (Job 38:4–5, 28–29, 37; 39:19, 26).

Through Job, God exhorts us to accept the fact that we do not have all the answers to the mysteries of the universe because we are not He. That means that natural disasters do have a place in God's plan, which we call His permissive will, that is, what He permits to happen under His auspices — as opposed to what He desires to happen, which we call his perfect will.

God tolerates evil so that He may bring a greater good from it (Q23). From the pain of privation in lost life and lost property, there are a multitude of lessons that God can teach us if we open ourselves to Him in these desperate moments. These are the goods that grow out of evil.

5. *IF GOD IS OMNISCIENT, HOW CAN WE HAVE FREE WILL?*

What if I told you that I knew you were going to open this book today and read this very question? Did my foreknowledge of what you would do have any impact on you — did it force you to open the book? No, you had no idea of my foreknowledge because I exist independently of you. You acted freely; I did not influence your choice or force you to act.

God's *omniscience*, His capacity to know all there is to know, and our free will work similarly. God exists independent of us. As pure Being, He is equally present to all things — past, present, and future, which exist as products of His thought.

So, God knows what we will do at every moment because of who and what He is. But His knowledge has no impact on our choices, which we make freely. He neither compels our actions nor our wills, nor do He or His will exist in competition with us and our wills. Rather, He is most happy when we freely choose to love Him and to follow His commandments — just as every parent is pleased when his child completes a task on his own. Far from coercing our action, God allows us to act freely, for only with the gift of freedom do we have the ability to love Him, and loving God is the greatest thing we can do in this life.

6. *WHAT IS THE MEANING OF LIFE?*

The meaning of life is to fulfill the commandment of Jesus Christ: to love God above all things and to love other people as we love ourselves. To love is to will the good of another — it is a free choice. Love, therefore, is not a feeling, though romantic love often carries strong emotions with it. In fact, love can coincide with feelings of frustration or worry, since it often requires self-sacrifice, as, for example, when loving parents wake up in the middle of the night to tend to crying children or when loving children assist their elderly parents as they age. This view of love is directly contrary to prevailing notions in popular culture that define the meaning of life as "happiness," which really only means getting what we want. Rather, Catholics know that in giving ourselves away to God and to others, we find true love and true happiness.

Other religions and philosophies offer their own meanings of life. It is worth comparing the Catholic view with that of the nonbeliever who thinks that life is an accidental product of evolution without an inherent purpose. If life is not designed by a higher Being, then it cannot have order and cannot make sense, because order and sense imply the working of some organizing principle. If this is true, then what we do — whether we act morally or not — has no purpose or consequences. Beware of the person who says, "I don't believe in God. I think all that matters in life is that I be a good person." How can there be a "good," and how can a person "be good," if there is no order nor purpose in the universe to define something as good?

Furthermore, when the meaning of life is defined only in material terms, that is, regarding only innate drives and physical things without reference to a higher power, that definition will fail to satisfy the human heart, which longs to love and to be loved. Only with a God who creates out of love and for love does life have meaning.

7. WHY SHOULD WE TRUST GOD EVEN WHEN IT ISN'T EASY?

Trust is a synonym of faith, and it is at the heart of any loving relationship. Acts of trust are ways we demonstrate our love. Every time we pray, attend Mass, or choose to obey God's commandments, we make acts of trust that God is real and that He is worth our efforts.

We can go deeper: if we are attentive in prayer, God can ask us to do all sorts of things that seem crazy or counter to what we desire. Yet He asks us to put our concerns into His hands and follow Him without fear. He did this with Abraham, whom God called at age seventy-five to leave his land of Haran and travel "to the land that I will show you" (Gen. 12:1). It is nearly impossible for us to imagine how dramatic this must have been for Abraham — to leave behind his entire life at such an advanced age and go to some unknown place, simply because God asked. But he did it. For Abraham's supreme act of trust, we rightly call him our father in faith, for, as God promised, his faith has reverberated through countless generations.

Similarly, Jesus called His apostles one or two at a time, repeating the command, "Follow me." To drop everything and follow Him can be terrifying, but God promises to reward us for our fidelity to Him: "Every one who has left houses or brothers or sisters or father or mother or children or lands, for my name's sake, will receive a hundredfold, and inherit eternal life" (Matt. 19:29).

CHAPTER 2

CATHOLICS AND SCIENCE

✝

8. *DON'T THE MIRACLES IN THE BIBLE CONTRADICT SCIENCE?*

Miracles that occur in the natural order — inexplicable actions of nature, the disappearance of deadly diseases — demonstrate God's power over everything He has created. Science is a measuring tool invented by finite human beings; therefore, it has limitations and cannot be the final authority on what is real and what is not. On rare occasions, God suspends the laws that He created to govern the universe in order to reassure us in our faith in Him. It is noteworthy that these miracles transcend the limits of nature rather than contradict them: there are no reported miracles of dirt being made into animals or of men being turned into dogs, as happens in fantasy novels. In transcending the limits of nature — restoring sight to the blind, walking on water, parting the Red Sea, making the sun dance in the sky (such as what transpired at Fatima, Portugal, in 1917) — miracles remind us that it is science, not God, that is limited in this world.

It is worth adding that science, as a discipline that studies the world, could not be performed if the universe were not ordered so precisely that it works according to discernible laws and patterns. That is, science exists because God created a world that can be measured. Just as human beings are not accidents (Q6), the universe is not an accident of random occurrences that are the antithesis of science. So, though a scientist may claim to be an atheist, practically speaking, in order for him to function as a scientist, he has to be a theist.

The biblical authors include miracles because they, and the witnesses of God's wondrous works, were amazed by what they saw: God intervening in time to alter the normal course of events. The keen, vivid details with which these miracles are described point toward their veracity: the events made such an impression that they were passed on to posterity in their fullness. (For more on the veracity of Jesus' miracles, see Q64.)

9. DOES THE THEORY OF EVOLUTION CONTRADICT THE BIBLE?

No. First of all, scientific theories cannot contradict the Bible because truth cannot contradict truth. If a perceived conflict should arise, then either the science or the Bible needs to be reinterpreted. But this perceived conflict is often overblown.

For example, when the sun, not the earth, was discovered to be at the center of the universe, it was thought that biblical interpretations that put the earth at the center had to be revised. In reality, all that had to be realized is that the earth is the spiritual center, not the geographic center, of the universe, as it is where God interacts with His people. So, there was no real conflict between science and the Bible on this issue, as critics of the Bible often allege.

On the other side, scientific discoveries can often lend rational credence to faith, as the big bang theory of the universe's creation seems to point to God as the Creator who initiated that bang. It is worth noting, however, that in the mid-twentieth century the Church resisted calls to declare the big bang theory definitive proof of God's Creation because she realized that science is always shifting and developing. God's revelation, by contrast, is fixed and does not depend on human measurements for its truth.

Regarding evolution itself, the theory does not contradict the idea of God as Creator for four reasons. First, as we already mentioned, the law of causality holds that for life to exist, God must exist to set it in motion; life does not come from nothing (Q2).

Second, God's primary manner of directing the universe is through natural causes: the planets move according to fixed forces at a fixed speed, the human body's nine systems all function according to their own internal regulations, new life comes into existence through reproduction. In directing the development of life, God could use any natural element that He wanted, including evolution of one species to another.

Third, the exact mechanism of evolution is unknown. Charles Darwin famously postulated random variation through natural selection, meaning that unplanned mutations caused changes in an organism which were passed on to offspring in a way that prompted a change into a whole other kind of organism. What Darwin and his followers call unplanned mutations is a philosophical judgment, not a scientific fact. What seems unplanned to us may just as easily be a development directed by God's invisible power. Moreover, unplanned mutations cannot by themselves harmonize into the fine-tuned order of animal bodies, and especially human bodies, so evolution on its own cannot account for the development of one species into another healthy one.

Fourth, evolution itself cannot account for the incredible differences between human beings and the primates closest to them. That the latter do not wonder about nor write about whether God exists shows just how dramatically human beings, as rational creatures, differ from their non-rational counterparts. Rationality is not a product of evolution; it signifies the presence of an immaterial rational soul that is implanted in each person directly by God (Q14).

God is the author of all that exists, and we are free to speculate how He does so. Evolution may well be the way God has created. In this sense, evolution should be viewed as proof of God's existence rather than evidence against it.

10. WHY IS THE CHURCH AGAINST IN VITRO FERTILIZATION (IVF)?

God gave human beings the gift of marriage through which we participate in His plan for the universe through procreation. IVF (in vitro fertilization) is wrong and sinful because it morphs procreation from an act of love between spouses — an act that is part of God's plan — into a laboratory experiment that involves multiple parties (and large amounts of money).

Rather than attempting to heal infertility, IVF circumvents bodily health entirely through a complicated process that includes immoral steps within itself. First, men masturbate into cups and women allow their eggs to be harvested. Next, third parties put these cells together in a laboratory to make multiple tiny human beings and then advise parents on which nascent lives hold the most potential. The embryos judged to be the healthiest are implanted; the others are either discarded (killed) or frozen indefinitely.

Although some believe that IVF is a pro-life action, that is not the case. IVF manufactures and manipulates defenseless human life as if it were a commodity to be sold. In IVF, the tiny embryos are treated like "clumps of cells," which is a phrase abortion advocates employ to justify killing a child in the womb. Children are one of God's greatest blessings, but we must never pursue good by evil means.

On the other hand, God does bring good out of evil. Children conceived through IVF are not accidents. These children are loved by God, who has endowed each one with a soul and has a plan for their lives.

Married couples experiencing the cross of infertility suffer greatly. For reasons we will never understand, God, the author of life, asks some couples to find their sanctification not through children but in other ways. He asks them to follow Him along the path to Calvary in faith. It is a path of sorrow, as it was for Him, yet somehow it leads to redemption.

11. WHAT DOES THE CHURCH TEACH ABOUT STEM-CELL RESEARCH, HUMAN CLONING, AND HUMAN-GENOME EDITING?

Let us first identify a few key principles that govern the Church's teachings on biotechnology. First, the Church fully supports scientific research aimed at improving the quality of human life so long as the methods and outcomes follow the moral law.

Second, human life can never be deliberately hurt or destroyed in pursuit of or in applying any technology or any medical advancement.

Third, the goal of each biotechnical application must be discerned before proceeding with it. Provided the techniques are moral, the Church approves of biotechnology that heals diseases and ailments; she also approves of biotechnology that strengthens health, such as, for example, the making of vitamins or nutrient supplements. The Church prohibits biotechnical applications that alter human beings' genetic or physical compositions in such a way that they become, in some respect, different from a "normal person." These applications, often called "enhancements" in popular discourse, undermine the dignity of the human person because they seek to change a person fundamentally, which implies that the person is a lesser being whose dignity depends not on God but on achieving a certain physical or chemical status.

Now let us consider the specific aspects of scientific study and research outlined in the question:

✠ *Stem cells* are human cells that exist within bodily organs to repair damaged tissues. Research has found that stem cells can be grown in labs to develop into other types of cells that can help overcome certain diseases. There are two types of stem cells: those that come from adult cells and those that come from human embryos. The Church fully supports experimentation with adult stem cells, for the person donating the cells is not harmed by doing so. The Church opposes research on stem cells that come from human embryos because the research results in destroying the embryos, which means the death of those human lives. The potential benefits of embryonic stem-cell research can never justify the destruction of human life.

✠ *Human cloning* is wrong and sinful because, as with IVF, it attempts to make human beings masters, rather than participants and cooperators, in God's plan of creation. Attempting to generate human life through cloning, whether to manufacture a new person or to cultivate cells for curing diseases, demotes the transmission of human life from an act of love to a heartless lab experiment.

✠ Ultimately, the giving of life is God's decision, not ours. Human life is not meant to be manipulated or controlled by others as a master owns a slave. But when human life is created in a lab, then the scientist functions as the master and the potential human lives are treated coldly as his property. Hence human cloning is a grave offense against the dignity of the human person.

✠ *Human-genome editing* refers to altering human DNA, a practice done using CRISPR (clustered regularly interspaced short palindromic repeats) gene-editing technology. The goal of gene editing must be established first to judge whether it is licit. The Church upholds the use of gene editing to cure diseases. As with stem-cell research, gene editing can occur morally only with an adult's cooperation; it is forbidden to use embryonic cells for gene-editing purposes. The Church opposes any gene editing that would alter a person's nature, be it his physical features or mental prowess, for such methods reject God and His plan for creation.

In sum, assuming moral means, biotechnologies that restore a human being from injury to wholeness are morally good; those that alter a human being's nature in any way are immoral.

12. WHY DO WE NEED GOD IF SCIENCE AND TECHNOLOGY CAN FIX ALL OUR PROBLEMS?

Science and technology are wonderful gifts that showcase human ingenuity, a power that comes from God. The scientific community has generated amazing material advances that have transformed the way we live and solved all sorts of difficulties. But they are limited to the material order; they cannot speak to human beings' spiritual needs — to our hearts and our desires for love, for relationships, for virtue, for goodness, for achievement. Only God can meet these needs.

Technology in itself is morally neutral, yet its alluring capabilities can exasperate spiritual problems by diverting our attention from them. Science and technology can fix our material problems, but if our hearts ache, only God can help us.

13. WHY DOESN'T GOD INTERVENE TO HELP US FIX THE WORLD'S PROBLEMS?

He does — to the degree that we cooperate with Him as stewards of creation.

As we saw in the first chapter, love is the greatest gift that God gives us, and it is contingent on our freedom to choose. If God were to intervene directly to fix the world's problems — wipe out poverty, rid the world of disease, end scarcity of food and goods — He would impinge upon both the order of the universe He created and upon our personal freedom.

We all know the difference, for example, between a real apology and a coerced one; we appreciate the former and despise the latter because sincerity makes the apology real and sincerity is an act of freedom. God wants us to fix the world's problems because in doing so we exercise the freedom He gave us and we express our love of Him through our works for others.

God also intervened to help us through the Incarnation of His Son, Jesus Christ, who enhances our abilities to fix the problems of the world by giving us His grace. These problems would be fixed more easily if more people would open themselves to

Christ and spread His love to others. This returns us to the first point: to solve the world's problems, we need more men and women to choose to follow Christ.

CHAPTER 3

HUMAN LIFE AND LIFE ON OTHER PLANETS

†

14. HOW IS A HUMAN SOUL DIFFERENT FROM THAT OF OTHER LIVING CREATURES?

The soul is the animating principle of a body, that is, the living quality that makes an organism alive. Dead bodies are dead because they no longer have their souls, which separate from bodies upon death. In this sense, both humans and animals have souls.

The human soul differs from that of animals in two crucial respects. First, the soul is pure spirit, meaning it is not made of physical matter. As such, it comes from God and can only come from God, a pure spirit; physical matter cannot produce something purely spiritual. Second, the human soul has two powers that make human beings different from all other animals: it has the ability to reason and the ability to will. Reasoning and willing are spiritual powers that are neither the product of human biology nor of evolution, though they are expressed through the body's actions. Loving, painting, designing, planning, and sacrificing are all acts of human rationality and will that other animals cannot do. The soul makes these actions possible.

The *Catechism of the Catholic Church* offers a helpful definition of the human soul that brings all its constitutive elements together: "The spiritual principle of human beings. The soul is the subject of human consciousness and freedom; soul and body together form one unique human nature. Each human soul is individual and immortal, immediately created by God. The soul does not die with the body, from which it is separated by death, and with which it will be reunited in the final resurrection" (*CCC* glossary).

15. *COULD A ROBOT WITH ARTIFICIAL INTELLIGENCE (AI) EVER HAVE A SOUL?*

No. The *A* of AI answers the question for us: it is *artificial* intelligence, that is, man-made or synthetic. The intelligent bot does not have independence; it receives its seeming intellectual powers from programmers who create the parameters within which it can work. No matter how powerful or "lifelike" AI seems, it does not have a soul, which possesses a natural freedom that no AI bot could ever have. Without freedom, AI is also incapable of the highest expression of human action: it cannot love. By contrast, the soul is an immaterial reality immediately created by God, not with human hands.

16. *DOES THE CHURCH SUPPORT TRANSHUMANISM?*

No. *Transhumanism* is the belief that human beings should employ technology to alter their nature. It is sometimes called *posthumanism*, a term that puts a stronger accent on changing human beings into some other kind of being. These changes may alter human cells to create bodies capable of living radically longer lives and intellects with cognition skills that radically exceed normal capacities. Transhumanism is a hubristic philosophy that rejects human nature as God intended it. This position is fundamentally different from human beings trying to reach higher levels of what they do naturally — run, jump, throw, climb, swim. It inherently rejects God as the author of creation by using technology to engineer a new type of creation.

17. DO ALIENS EXIST – AND IF SO, WOULD THEY NEED TO BE SAVED?

There is no official Church teaching concerning aliens or life on other planets. If aliens do exist on other planets, then they, like everything on earth, were made by God and will find their fulfillment in Him. If intelligent life equivalent to human life exists, we do not know whether it would need to be saved, for we would have to discern its relationship to God first. We do know that other intelligent life would not jeopardize nor attenuate human beings' unique relationship with God. Human beings are privileged to be made in God's image and likeness and to be saved by Him.

18. HOW DO WE KNOW THAT HUMAN LIFE IS NOT AN ACCIDENT?

Human beings are not a cosmic accident. Everything that exists is willed by God. What is willed by God is good and has meaning. God, who is not limited by space and time as we are, is equally present to and cares for all of creation, from the galaxies and planets down to the microscopic organisms. Nothing is trivial or insignificant to Him. Jesus reassured His disciples that "even the hairs of your head are all numbered. Fear not, therefore; you are of more value than many sparrows" (Matt. 10:30–31).

Moreover, human beings are the crown of God's creation, for we alone were created for a personal and everlasting relationship with Him. That is, we were made to live in God's love, so He cares about everything we do, even more than a parent, spouse, or friend would care. The prophet Isaiah expressed this best: "For the mountains may depart and the hills be removed, but my steadfast love shall not depart from you, and my covenant of peace shall not be removed, says the LORD, who has compassion on you" (Isa. 54:10).

Since human beings are by nature purposeful, that is, everything they do is for a purpose, it is hard to imagine that such beings are the product of a grand accident rather than a purposeful plan. In other words, we cannot be purposeful beings if there were not a broader purpose for our existence. Accidents do not generate purpose.

No, human beings are not accidents, and neither is your life nor my life. God created each of us with a purpose: to live in a loving relationship with Him here on earth and then forever in Heaven.

19. WOULD WE NEED TO REINTERPRET THE BIBLE IF OTHER LIFE FORMS ARE FOUND?

No. All of creation, even the parts we don't yet know about, proclaims God's glory. Psalm 19 succinctly expresses this mystery: "The heavens are telling the glory of God; and the firmament proclaims his handiwork" (Ps. 19:1).

Throughout history, human beings have learned more and more about the mysteries of the cosmos. We know more in the twenty-first century than we did in the twentieth, when we knew more than in the nineteenth, and so on. More knowledge and greater scientific power have only enhanced our wonder at God's omnipotent creativity.

For example, though the latest scientific research postulates that millions of theoretically habitable planets exist within our galaxy, as far as we know, one and only one planet contains life: earth. The existence of life as we know it on earth has overcome infinitesimally small odds, a fact that affirms the Bible's revelation of a God who deliberately chose to create something extremely special: life on earth.

CHAPTER 4

GOD, GOOD, AND EVIL

†

20. *IF GOD IS GOOD, WHY DO EVIL AND INJUSTICE EXIST?*

Love is the greatest force in the universe because God is love (1 John 4:8). To love, that is, to will the good of another, freedom is required. But freedom is not truly free unless it has the capacity to choose the good. God gives us this power because in choosing the good we choose Him, and in choosing Him we show our love for Him.

To understand our freedom to choose the good, consider this analogy: A school schedules a "Christmas boutique" so its youngest students can purchase gifts for their family members. A boy tells his father of the boutique and asks for money. The father gives the boy ten dollars and this instruction: "You may buy one gift for your mother and one for your sister." The next day, the boy goes to school with the ten dollars. At lunch, he decides to use the money to buy ice cream for himself. Then, at the boutique, he sees something he really likes and buys it for himself. With that purchase, he ran out of money.

In choosing to spend the money on himself rather than on the gifts as his father had requested, the boy violated the tenets of his freedom. That is, rather than choose the good for which his freedom was ordered, he chose wrongly, for with freedom comes the responsibility to use it correctly. From his wrong choice, evil follows. Where evil exists, injustice follows immediately thereafter.

Adam and Eve, the first human beings, violated their freedom by choosing to follow their own desires over God's will. This is called Original Sin, and it disrupted the order of creation that God had intended. As a result, evil became a reality in our world in two kinds: natural evil, the diseases, disabilities, and natural disasters that are part of the universe; and moral evil, the wrong actions that human beings do.

Moreover, Original Sin has stained human nature with an innate tendency toward evil that is called *concupiscence*. As a result, human beings, though created good, exist in a fallen state with disordered desires, a clouded intellect, and a weakened will that often are enticed to choose evil rather than good. So evil and injustice will continue to exist in the world until the end of time.

Christ gives us His own divine power to resist our tendency toward evil and choose the good instead. This divine power is called *grace*, and it is communicated chiefly, but not exclusively, through the sacraments.

Life on earth, therefore, is a constant battle between good and evil. Through faith, though, we know that good will triumph at the end of time because the universe and all of creation belong to God.

21. *IS EVERYTHING EVIL ALSO A SIN?*

A sin is a deliberate choice to do what is evil. As such, sin is a rejection of God who loves us and bids us to choose the good. We reject God when we willingly violate His commandments. While every sin is evil, there are some evils that are not sins because they are not the result of a deliberate human choice. For example, if a man attentively driving his car inadvertently strikes and kills a child riding his bicycle, an evil has occurred with the death of the child. But the driver did not commit a sin because he was acting responsibly and he did not will to strike the child. It was an accident.

22. HOW CAN WE KNOW SOMETHING IS GOOD AND NOT EVIL?

There are two primary ways; one is through reason and the other through faith. Through reason, we know that what is good is what corresponds to nature, to logic, and to the purpose for which something is made. We can say this another way: what is good is what is true, and our knowledge is true when it matches how things exist in the world. Moral reasoning according to the way things are made is called natural law.

For example, a human being is born and exists freely in the world. To impinge upon his life — by killing him, by harming him, by enslaving him — is contrary to how human life ought to exist in nature; any such actions, therefore, are evil. Conversely, actions that help human beings to live well, such as aiding the poor or teaching the young, are good actions. Concerning the end for which something is made, marriage is an exclusive union of one man and one woman for the sake of family life. Adultery and divorce violate the purpose of marriage, so both actions are evil. Conversely, married couples do good when they bring children into the world.

The second way we know is through faith: God revealed what is good and evil in simple terms through the Ten Commandments. These are laws that are universal in their scope, meaning they are for all times and all places, not just for Jews or Christians. What is commanded to be done is good; what is forbidden is evil. They also help us judge whether scores of other actions are good or evil. For example, from the fifth commandment not to kill we know that abortion, harming oneself or others with drugs or alcohol, and damaging another person with insults or gossip are also evil. The actions commanded and forbidden also align perfectly with what human reason discerns about what is good and what is evil.

23. WHY DOESN'T GOD JUST ELIMINATE EVIL?

Evil is the great scourge of human existence. Everyone hates it and wishes it would disappear, even as each person, to one degree or another, is responsible for evil in the world by his sins.

The existence of evil in the world is a great mystery, and we are limited in our ability to understand beyond what God has revealed to us in the Bible. We find a hint of an explanation to this question in the parable of the weeds among the wheat (Matt. 13:24–30): A man sowed good seed into the soil, but at night an enemy came and sowed weeds among the wheat; the weeds and wheat then grew intertwined in the soil. The servants ask their master if they should pluck out the weeds. The master forcefully responds, "No; lest in gathering the weeds you root up the wheat along with them. Let both grow together until the harvest; and at harvest time I will tell the reapers, 'Gather the weeds first and bind them in bundles to be burned, but gather the wheat into my barn'" (29–30).

We live in the time of the growing season; the harvest is the end of the world. So we must deal with the reality of evil — the weeds — for God has allowed it to grow alongside the good. As we have already said, for freedom and love to exist, the possibility of evil must exist as well (Q20).

Despite the harsh reality of evil, Catholics take comfort in two facts that God has revealed. First, we could not have so great a Savior in Jesus Christ if there were not evil from which we must be saved.

Hence the Church at the Easter Vigil sings, "O happy fault [of Adam] that earned so great, so glorious a Redeemer!" Moreover, our Savior is not unfamiliar with evil's scourge: He experienced it in all its dark ferocity on the Cross.

Second, God does not will evil; He tolerates the evil that we, His creatures, do. Because the universe belongs to Him, He will bring good out of every evil, even if we cannot always see the good or must suffer as we wait for it.

24. WHY DOES GOD ALLOW PEOPLE TO SUFFER, EVEN BABIES AND CHILDREN?

Suffering is part of the human condition as a result of sin. Whether our sufferings are comparatively light, such as having a minor illness or dealing with unpleasant neighbors, or they are far heavier to endure, such as losing a job, a home, a loved one, or experiencing debilitating illnesses, we abhor suffering and pray to God to lift it from us.

Even though we can feel as if God has abandoned us in our suffering, we know that God is not deaf to our concerns. His love for us works in ways that we cannot imagine. Rather than take away all suffering, He became a man to suffer along with us — and because of us. All the pains we encounter in this life, be they physical, emotional, or spiritual, God Himself has experienced through the Incarnation. By His Passion and death, Christ teaches us that accepting suffering willingly is the way to redemption.

Redemptive suffering is easy to speak about but terribly difficult to endure. It requires God's help and repeated, concerted efforts on our parts to redirect our sufferings from looking in on ourselves to looking up toward God. In doing so, we tell God in prayer that we will bear the pain, as Jesus did, for the sake of our salvation and that of others. Catholics call this "offering up" our sufferings. Doing so does not take our pain away; it makes us better able to tolerate it and, better still, to make it meaningful and salvific in our lives.

Nonbelievers often point to suffering in the world as proof that there is no God. They fail to see that in human sufferings God is right there next to us, every step of the way. Our limited minds cannot comprehend how, in God's plan that tolerates evil for a greater good, bad things happen to good people. Such happenings disrupt our innate sense of justice, and yet through our suffering, God teaches us some of the most important — and difficult — lessons of human life: we must cease trying to control every aspect of our lives and must learn to trust Him by following wherever He leads us.

25. *IS SATAN REAL? WHAT ABOUT DEMONS?*

Yes. Satan and demons are real. Page after page of the Bible speaks of their existence, and Jesus mentions Satan repeatedly; He even battles against him during His forty-day fast in the desert. In fact, the Gospels convey that Jesus was not merely teaching us how to live; He was engaging in a cosmic battle against the forces of evil present in the world.

Satan and the demons were all created angels when they, by their own free will, rejected God. Their rejection was total: they remain forever opposed to God and the good that He does in the universe. Satan, also called the devil or Lucifer, is the leader of these demons, these fallen angels. The name *Satan* means "the Accuser," which describes how he works: he accuses us of our sins to make us feel guilty with the goal of leading us away from God and into despair, which is his province.

Since Satan and his demons are consumed by evil and hate the good, they work by tempting us to choose evil. They do this in any number of ways, but their most effective means is to deceive us into believing that what is truly evil is somehow good; thus, we do not feel as if we are doing wrong. The more evil we do, the more we give ourselves to Satan's power.

Satan and demons are not equal to God, who has dominion over them. Although they are not limited by space and time and so can appear to tempt us at a moment's notice, they are not privy to our private thoughts the way God is.

Satan's power can induce fear in us, but if we live close to Christ, follow the commandments, pray often, and make regular use of the Sacrament of Penance, he stands little chance of making inroads against us.

26. WHAT HAPPENS IF MY CONSCIENCE TELLS ME TO DO SOMETHING EVIL?

Conscience is the inner forum of a human being's heart where he discerns God's law, which is inscribed within him. It contains two elements: the perception of God's law and the judgment of whether a particular action is good or evil.

Because part of conscience includes perception of what is good and what is evil, all human beings must form their consciences over the course of their lives (*CCC* 1784) so they can correctly perceive the difference between good and evil. Conscience is formed through study and through prayer; the former includes reading fiction and watching films in addition to engaging educational texts. Learning and praying about God's law through reading the Bible and the *Catechism of the Catholic Church* and listening to homilies and Catholic podcasts effectively develop the conscience.

Because the conscience is intimately personal, it is wrong for another person or entity to force a person to violate his conscience; it is also wrong to forbid a person to act according to his conscience (CCC 1782). For example, the government cannot coerce citizens to worship a certain deity, nor can it coerce them to perform an action that is a sin; it also cannot forbid a person from worshipping God.

In addition, because the conscience is the inner core of a human being, a person is obliged to follow his conscience, that is, his judgment about whether an action is good or evil; to act against his conscience would be to contradict himself. This fact does not justify the choice of an evil action, however. The person is responsible for his judgment, so if his conscience tells him to do evil, he has done evil; the judgment of conscience cannot transform an evil act into a good one.

The degree to which a person's conscience is formed can mitigate the guilt of someone who does an evil action. For example, an adult who since youth was taught that stealing is good still commits evil if he steals something because he acts contrary to the nature of things and to God's law. But his guilt is less than that of someone who has been taught that stealing is wrong yet does it anyway.

Similarly, choosing to believe in and follow Jesus Christ as God is a judgment of conscience; a person is not culpable for not choosing to follow Christ if he through no fault of his own has not heard of Him. But a person who has heard of Christ is responsible for his decision not to believe in Him. In other words, "I was just following my conscience" never justifies an evil action.

CHAPTER 5

MORALITY AND SIN

†

27. *WHY SHOULD I FOLLOW CHURCH TEACHING WHEN OTHERS DON'T?*

The teachings of the Church come from Christ; we follow the teachings according to His command and for His sake, not simply to please any other authority figure such as a priest or parent.

Christ appointed His apostles and their successors, the bishops, to serve as our leaders and teachers and to pass on to us faithfully the teachings of the Church. Likewise, He commands us to obey those upon whom He has bestowed this authority. And yet, the Church and her teachings do not belong to the bishops, but to Christ. So even if they do not follow Jesus' teachings, we must still do what is right because we are followers of Christ.

During His earthly ministry, Jesus was keenly aware of the damage that religious leaders who fail to live up to what they profess can cause. He excoriated the Pharisees, the Jewish leaders of His day, for their hypocrisy. He called them blind fools, serpents, a brood of vipers, and whitewashed tombs. Nevertheless, He instructed His disciples to obey them: "The scribes and the Pharisees sit on Moses' seat; so practice and observe whatever they tell you" (Matt. 23:2–3). We obey bishops and priests because of their office, not because of who they are as individuals or how they behave. Jesus is clear: do what they say, not what they do, for what they say are His very words of spirit and life that lead us to Him.

28. WHY DOES BEING MORAL MATTER?

Morality refers to whether an action is good or evil. An action is moral if it is good and immoral if it is evil. As we have already noted (Q22), an action is good if it corresponds to the truth of nature, of logic, of purpose, and of the divine law that God revealed; an action is evil if it transgresses any of these standards.

Being moral matters because the very drama of human life is to do good and avoid evil. Epics, novels, movies, and television shows all convey this: excitement comes from the pursuit of the good and avoidance of evil. The "happy ending" that we all desire is the choice of the good, simply because the good truly satisfies us. God made us for the good, that is, for Himself. Living a moral life leads us to Him, and He is our true happiness.

Today many believe that morality cannot be known because there is no universal agreement on what is good or evil. Therefore, an action can be "right for you" but "wrong for me." This belief is called *moral relativism*, and it is a great scourge of our time, since it falsely leads people to assume there is no truth and that their actions do not matter.

The lack of agreement concerning what is good or evil does not negate the reality that actions are, in themselves, good or evil according to nature, logic, purpose, and God. Frankly, lack of agreement on moral questions often stems from a rebellious human will that seeks to rationalize evil actions by calling them good. Acceptance of an objective good and evil are required to condemn Hitler's actions as evil and to proclaim Martin Luther King's civil rights efforts as good.

Moreover, a just human society cannot exist if moral relativism is the norm; the entire criminal justice system hinges on certain actions being defined as evil and therefore forbidden. If we consider that so many different societies have considered the same types of actions morally evil — murder, theft, adultery, destruction of persons or property — we realize that underpinning these legal decisions is an authentic human understanding of what is good and what is evil according to the order of creation.

Christ entrusted the Church with His teachings about morality and the human person so that we may know better how to live in His love. The Church, therefore, urges her children to live a moral life as Christ commanded, for only that leads to union with God.

29. IS ANY SIN TRULY UNFORGIVABLE?

Jesus told the crowds following Him, "Truly, I say to you, all sins will be forgiven the sons of men, and whatever blasphemies they utter; but whoever blasphemes against the Holy Spirit never has forgiveness, but is guilty of an eternal sin" (Mark 3:28–29).

Blasphemy against the Holy Spirit is the sin of final impenitence, that is, the sin of refusing God's love and mercy in the final moments of a person's life. It is one of the great mysteries of creation that God respects our freedom; He will never force us to accept Him. If a person stubbornly refuses to accept God even at the moment of death, this sin cannot be forgiven because the person never shows sorrow, which is necessary to receive God's forgiveness.

Whenever a person shows genuine sorrow for sin, God will forgive him. There are two types of sin: venial sins are less severe sins and typically done without proper consideration, while mortal sins are grave violations of the Ten Commandments done willingly and with full knowledge of the wrong (CCC 1857, 1862). Both types of sins are forgiven in the Sacrament of Penance, also known as Confession.

30. WHAT IF I THINK IT'S OKAY TO DO SOMETHING THE CHURCH SAYS IS WRONG?

We know that what the Church teaches concerning the moral life is true, for it is the teaching of Christ Himself. Therefore, if a person judges in conscience that it is good to do an action that the Church teaches is wrong, he does evil. One's personal opinion about an act — even if based on the judgment of conscience (Q26), cannot transform an evil act into a good one, nor does it justify performing an evil action.

It is a great tragedy of our time that God's laws and the Church's teachings are commonly perceived as inhibiting — rather than enhancing — human freedom. The Church's teachings function like parents guiding their children. Catholics would enrich their moral and spiritual lives by looking at God's law and Church teaching as gifts, not impositions, as King David sang in the psalms: "The law of the LORD is perfect, reviving the soul; the testimony of the LORD is sure, making wise the simple; the precepts of the LORD are right, rejoicing the heart; the commandment of the LORD is pure, enlightening the eyes" (Ps. 19:7–8).

31. IS IT A SIN TO BE RACIST?

Yes. To be a racist is to hate a person for how he looks or because of his heritage. Such hatred is directly contrary to Jesus' commandment to love our neighbor, who, according to the parable of the good Samaritan (Luke 10:29–37), is every person, regardless of birth or appearance.

All human beings are made in the image and likeness of God. As a result, simply by virtue of being created by God, all human beings have an innate dignity that no person may violate for any reason. To oppose or hate someone because of his race violates his dignity as a child of God and therefore is a sin.

32. WHY WOULD A LOVING GOD SEND A PERSON TO HELL?

St. Paul tells us that God "desires all men to be saved and to come to the knowledge of the truth" (1 Tim. 2:4). At the same time, Christ teaches that "He who believes and is baptized will be saved; but he who does not believe will be condemned" (Mark 16:16).

How do we balance these two statements? Belief is a choice, which means that we have the power to choose God by believing in Him or reject God by refusing to believe. If a person rejects God, he acts contrary to God's will that the person choose Him and be saved.

God, therefore, does not send anyone to Hell. Rather, a person chooses Hell for himself by refusing to believe in God and to follow His commandments. There is a strong logic to this: if Heaven is eternity with God, why would a person who freely rejected God in this life want to spend all eternity with Him? Hell is the permanent separation of the soul from God; it is the natural consequence of choosing to live on earth separated from God.

33. IS IT A SIN TO PLAY WITH A OUIJA BOARD OR TO DABBLE IN THE OCCULT?

Yes. Using Ouija boards, using tarot cards, consulting psychic media, or using other means of summoning hidden powers, including Wicca and other forms of witchcraft or occult practices, are serious sins because they invite the forces of evil into a person's life while showing disdain for God. These practices are extremely dangerous, as they enable evil to come into our souls; their use can even contribute to demonic possession.

Curiosity is never an excuse to commit a sin. The Church teaches that any involvement in or use of any witchcraft or any occult practices must be confessed to a priest, who may advise further sacramental and prayer measures to make sure the person is free of all demonic presence.

CHAPTER 6

HUMAN SEXUALITY

†

34. WHY DOES THE CHURCH PROHIBIT SEX OUTSIDE OF MARRIAGE?

God creates because He wishes to share His love with us. Through procreation, God invites us to share in His love more intimately, as the love of a man and a woman generates new human life. By continuing and ordering creation through us, God entrusts us with an awesome responsibility: to further His plan by cooperating with His will.

Through the gift of human sexuality, we have the ability to generate new life. Because this new life needs tremendous quantities of love and attention over many years, sex belongs within a committed marriage. The sexual instinct and the innate human need for love and for relationship find their natural fulfillment in marriage, where couples come together for the sake of forming a new family.

By perpetuating a destructive lie that separates sex and reproduction, secular culture has undermined marriage and family life for decades. Divorce, absentee parents, childhood abuse and neglect, abortion, sexual exploration, and sexual exploitation are the rotten fruits of this lie. The physical pleasure of sex cannot be isolated from its reproductive nature without harming the most vulnerable.

Marriage is God's great gift to men and women, for the love of husband and wife for each other and their children is an image of the

Holy Trinity's love. Hence it is only within marriage that sex is fully realized as a life-giving act.

35. WHAT'S WRONG WITH LIVING WITH A ROMANTIC PARTNER?

Marriage is the only relationship worthy of the sexual act's twofold significance of procreation and of expressing love. Marriage alone is worthy because the love of the spouses is free, total, faithful, and fruitful. Within the marital union, a husband and wife each promise, voluntarily and without coercion, to give his or her entire self to the other. Each promises to love the other, and only the other, until death; and marital love is to overflow into new life.

When a boyfriend and girlfriend move in with each other, their relationship lacks these four dimensions of love. Since they are not married, their union is neither total nor faithful — either person could leave at any moment without consequence. Because of the impermanence of this relationship, many choose to use contraception to avoid having children, or run the risk of becoming single parents. And even though cohabitation may be their choice, they lack the peace of a couple who freely commits to a vowed marriage.

In other words, cohabitation is wrong and sinful because it is a poor imitation of marriage. It plagiarizes marriage's grandeur by distorting the nature of the sexual act and deprives the man and the woman of the blessings that follow from having a spouse who loves him or her freely, totally, faithfully, and fruitfully.

36. *WHAT'S WRONG WITH CONTRACEPTION?*

The procreative and unitive aspects of sex cannot be separated because marriage, as noted in the prior question, demands a love that is free, total, faithful, and fruitful. To use artificial contraception, even within a marriage, is to shortchange the love between spouses. That is, the love expressed in a contracepted sexual act is not total — the spouse is withholding his or her fertility and therefore is not giving fully of himself or herself. The act is also not fruitful, as the spouses have intentionally removed the possibility of having children; their love, rather than potentially overflowing outwardly to new life, has been willfully sterilized and closed in on itself.

It is not the case that every sexual act can or must result in children. There are situations of health or finance that may cause couples to postpone having children for years or even indefinitely. Couples can avoid pregnancy naturally by abstaining during the wife's fertile periods; this practice is called *natural family planning* (NFP).

NFP is very different from artificial contraception, for it works according to the order of human sexuality that God created; a wife's periodic infertility is part of that order. When couples engage in the marital act during that time, they are cooperating with this natural order. By contrast, artificial contraception rejects this order by deliberately thwarting it.

As previously noted (Q28), living a moral life leads to God and brings a degree of peace for knowingly walking along the path He made for us. This applies equally to adhering to God's plan for human sexuality. Human beings will always do better to live according to God's plan than to devise their own moral path, which will, despite even sincere intentions, lead not to fulfillment but to dissatisfaction or ruin.

37. WHAT'S WRONG WITH MASTURBATION?

As mentioned previously (Q34–36), the procreative powers are meant to be the expression of married love that is free, total, faithful, and fruitful. Masturbation is wrong and a sin because it reduces the procreative powers to an urge that a person seeks to relieve. The sexual act is meant to be a life-giving act; masturbation is a selfish act.

There is no such thing as a private sin. Each time we choose ourselves over God, we turn in on ourselves and become weaker and more inclined to yield to the next temptation. Sexual temptation, like all other temptations, must be resisted with the help of God's grace and the cultivation of chastity, which is the virtue that regulates the sexual instinct so that it remains part of a person without controlling him. St. John Paul II described chastity as the "spiritual energy capable of defending love from the perils of selfishness and aggressiveness, and able to advance it towards its full realization."[1]

38. WHAT'S WRONG WITH WATCHING PORNOGRAPHY?

Pornography exploits and demeans the gift of human sexuality. It ensnares and wounds everyone involved, from those who produce and distribute it to those who watch it. Pornography perverts the sexual act, which is meant to be private, from an act of love into a public act of exploitation. It is always a serious sin.

It is wrong and a sin to watch pornography for several reasons. First, the viewer derives sexual pleasure from illicit sexual activity that he should have no part in. Second, patronizing pornography

---

[1]   John Paul II, Apostolic Exhortation on the Role of the Christian Family in the Modern World *Familiaris Consortio* (November 22, 1981), no. 33.

encourages the making and distributing of these materials, perpetuating the exploitation and abuse. Third, pornography damages the viewer psychologically: it generates unrealistic understandings of what sex is, it distorts the experience of sex with one's spouse, and it can become an addiction that is difficult to break. This makes watching pornography not only sinful but also dangerous for the viewer's mental health and for the proper exercise of his sexuality in marriage.

39. IS ABORTION EVER NECESSARY?

No. Life is a precious gift from God, and it must always be treated as such, even when doing so requires suffering and sacrifice on our part. Abortion, the deliberate killing of a human life, rejects God's gift. It is therefore never necessary or justified.

Abortions occur in two ways: chemically (by means of pills) or surgically (by means of instruments). The "abortion pill" contains mifepristone and misoprostol, which prevent a newly fertilized human embryo from implanting in his mother's womb and then forces contractions to expel him from her body, killing him. A surgical abortion dismembers the child inside his mother's womb and then extracts him via the birth canal. These hideous practices are never necessary for any reason. The direct taking of an innocent human life is murder, which is always evil and can never be justified.

Pregnancy is fraught with dangers, and newly conceived lives are incredibly fragile. Tragically, abortion supporters have exploited this sad fact under the banner of "saving the life of the mother" as a tool to push for abortion's legality.

However, proper health care, even for the most difficult pregnancy-related emergencies, cares for both mother and child. Abortion treats a child in utero not as a person deserving care but as a disease to be destroyed. Proper health care never does evil so that good may come of it.

Proper health care also is aware of its limits: not every pregnancy can be saved, despite our best efforts. For example, ectopic pregnancies, when the fertilized embryo implants in the fallopian tube, always result in miscarriage. Proper health care recognizes the human dignity of the tiny embryo, and when possible, waits for it to resolve naturally by passing out of the tube and through the birth canal. However, should the mother develop an infection, doctors are permitted morally to treat the infection by removing the tube, which results indirectly in the sad death of the child. That child, like other miscarried or stillborn babies, may be interred in a cemetery; most Catholic cemeteries have special sections for such burials.

The moral intricacies of ectopic pregnancies and other pregnancy issues can be challenging to comprehend and are outside the scope of this book. Whenever a person is unsure of the moral path to take, he should call his diocesan chancery or consult the website of the National Catholic Bioethics Center for guidance on how to act in a certain situation.

40. IS IT A SIN TO BE GAY?

No. Sexual attraction is innate and not sinful in itself, though it can lead to sin if not regulated appropriately.

Our age has wrongly made sexual attraction — now called "sexual identity" — into the defining characteristic of a person, and it refuses to acknowledge any limits on sexual activity. Rather, it lionizes "consent," meaning that if a person wants sex and finds another who agrees, then they may do whatever they want.

These views are wrong, for they reject the order of sexuality that God has established so that we may participate in His love in a profound way. They also advocate for men and women to be ruled by their passions instead of using reason to discern which actions are good and which are evil.

Sexuality is an important part of a person, but it is not the definitive part. It is important for all men and women to develop the virtue of chastity to regulate the sexual instinct, just as the virtue of temperance is necessary to regulate the appetite for eating and drinking. Regulation is not suppression as opponents of Catholic morality allege. Regulation is necessary for the proper development of the sexual instinct and its healthy use in the correct context: expression within the marital union and abstinence during other times.

Chastity is not a negative virtue. It allows for positive relationships with oneself and with others. As the Pontifical Council for the Family describes it,

> Chastity is the joyous affirmation of someone who knows how to live [in a] self-giving [manner], free from any form of self-centered slavery. This presupposes that the person has learnt how to accept other people, to relate with them, while respecting their dignity in diversity. The chaste person is not self-centered, not involved in selfish relationships with other people. Chastity makes the personality harmonious. It matures it and fills it with inner peace. This purity of mind and body helps develop true self-respect and at the same time makes one capable of respecting others, because it makes one see in them persons to

reverence, insofar as they are created in the image of God and through grace are children of God, re-created by Christ.[2]

Developing chastity is a challenge for all people. Men or women who experience same-sex attraction face an additional challenge because their instinct is disordered, that is, it is directed contrary to the nature of human sexuality. As such, same-sex attraction can never be acted upon, for same-sex acts are always wrong.

It is essential to acknowledge that a person experiencing same-sex attraction is loved by God and is entitled to the same love and respect as any other person. It is also essential to acknowledge that same-sex attraction cannot be considered good even though a person did not choose the attraction. In this regard, same-sex attraction can be better understood as a misfiring of the sexual instinct. Misfires are never good nor things to celebrate.

Sadly, today's world has pressured those experiencing same-sex attraction to embrace and celebrate it by adopting labels such as gay, lesbian, bisexual, or transgender to describe themselves. These terms and the lifestyles that the media have associated with them are contrary to the virtue of chastity because they allow sexual appetites to control the person and dictate the course of his life. The opposite should be the case: the virtue of chastity allows the person to accept his sexuality, wherever it may be oriented, and then govern it accordingly.

Men and women experiencing same-sex attraction often suffer greatly. They deserve the full help of God's grace working through the Church as well as the encouragement of family and friends to

[2]   Pontifical Council for the Family, *The Truth and Meaning of Human Sexuality* (December 8, 1995), no. 17.

remain chaste. Sometimes, for reasons we cannot understand, God asks some of His children to carry heavy crosses through life's most basic areas of health and relationships. For those understandably feeling overwhelmed by the weight of the cross of same-sex attraction, St. Paul's words could offer hope: "No temptation has overtaken you that is not common to man. God is faithful, and he will not let you be tempted beyond your strength, but with the temptation will also provide the way of escape, that you may be able to endure it" (1 Cor. 10:13). "My grace is sufficient for you, for my power is made perfect in weakness" (2 Cor. 12:9).

41. WHY DOES THE CHURCH PROHIBIT SAME-SEX MARRIAGE?

As mentioned previously (Q34–36), God created marriage as part of the natural order to carry on His plan of creation. He created men and women for each other and stamped their mutual dependency into their bodies. Of the nine systems of the human body, only the reproductive system is incomplete within a single person; it requires a person of the opposite sex to complete it. With the physiological complementarity comes sexual attraction so that men and women may enter into physical union to procreate. Marriage enshrines this union before God and before society to foster its fruit, children, who need the love and constant care of their mothers and their fathers in order to grow into healthy adults.

Same-sex marriage, therefore, is not possible because, by its nature, it is contrary to the purpose of marriage. The relationship of love that marriage includes is an inseparable complement to the order of procreation; a relationship of romantic love not physically ordered to procreation cannot be marital.

It is worth noting that the Catholic Church was the first to bring together the twin elements of marital love: procreation and strengthening the loving relationship of spouses. Before then, couples entered marriage for procreation as a means of uniting families, not for love. Today the Sexual Revolution demands the opposite: marriage for love, not for procreation. This is every bit a distortion of marriage as it is a denial of its loving element. The Church has done the world a great service by uniting procreation and love as the inseparable elements of marriage.

42. WHY CAN TWO STERILE PEOPLE MARRY BUT TWO GAY PEOPLE CANNOT?

As we have already stated, God created men and women to complement each other, and that complementarity is imprinted on their bodies. The sexual relations of married couples occur within a natural order that ties procreation together with strengthening the love between spouses. Even when age, disease, or timing prevent a married couple from conceiving a child, each time they come together they testify to that oneness and complementarity God intended. As already noted (Q36), not every sexual act by a married couple can or must result in procreation.

The sexual relations of two people of the same sex lack both the complementarity of God's design as well as any life-giving potential. In other words, they are contrary to the natural order. There is no comparison, therefore, between a sterile married couple and two people of the same sex. The former works according to nature and to human biology while the latter act against both.

43. WHY IS THE CHURCH AGAINST TRANSGENDERISM?

Transgenderism is the belief that a person's gender can be different from his biological sex. This is false for several reasons. First, to claim that a person's inner being differs from his physical being is by its very nature false because, as noted previously (Q22), truth is that which accords with nature, logic, and purpose. Just as it is impossible, for example, for the same thing to exist and not to exist at the same time and in the same place, so a person cannot physically be a man while also being a woman and vice versa.

Second, human beings are by nature embodied spirits, that is, their souls are intricately united to their bodies and cannot exist apart from them. Therefore, men are incapable of experiencing themselves and the world in any other way except as men, and the same goes for women. Any claims to the contrary are simply not possible.

Third, men and women have distinct physiological and psychological characteristics that are written into their DNA; in addition to differences in body type and reproduction, men and women's brains are structurally different. For a man, then, to claim he is a woman, is to contradict his entire self — mind, body, and spirit. It is impossible to change a person's sex. To claim that sex remains constant yet gender is a conscious choice that can change is false, for gender cannot be separated from embodied sexuality.

The Creation stories in the book of Genesis affirm what we learn from biology: that human beings are God's unique creation, different from all other animals and species. God created man and woman to complement each other; together they reflect His image. Male and female complementarity hinges on their distinct and innate differences.

A person is most fully himself when his mind, body, and spirit are properly integrated. Gender dysphoria is a real mental disorder that occurs when a man believes he is a woman or a woman believes she is a man, pitting a person's mind, body, and spirit against each other. It needs to be treated as a disorder so that, with proper counseling and medication, the person experiencing these symptoms may overcome them.

Any person suffering from gender dysphoria must be treated with love and respect by all those around him. However, claiming that this disorder is healthy, normal, or something that should be encouraged by hormonal therapy or surgical alteration (a form of mutilation, as explained in CCC 2297) is neither loving nor correct.

CHAPTER 7

CATHOLICISM, OTHER RELIGIONS, SPIRITUALITY, AND DOUBT

✝

44. WHY DO WE NEED RELIGION – CAN'T WE CONNECT TO GOD ON OUR OWN?

We need religion for several reasons. First, human beings are finite and fallible creatures. One person declaring his own personal truth as "my truth" — vis-à-vis other people and the world — on major questions of life is highly likely to err. The individual is strengthened when he wrestles with deeper questions and seeks God from within a group or a tradition.

Second, religion is natural to human beings. What is religion? It is a way of relating to God through specific practices and beliefs. Throughout history, religions have developed naturally within various cultures as ways to relate to the supernatural. Human beings are hardwired for God; worshipping the higher power is part of human nature. The highest form of worship is done collectively, as each community seeks to define its relationship before the Almighty.

Some secularists equate religion with mythology and claim that religion stems from the uneducated masses. They are wrong on both counts. Religion is an encounter with the divine and requires something from us; mythology rationalizes explanations for wondrous deeds and asks nothing of us.

Third, religion is more than a system of beliefs, as it is often reduced to in today's thinking. Religion includes beliefs about God but is more than that: it concerns our interaction with God. Because of this, religion was once a synonym for piety and devotion, though that view has tragically been lost today.

Catholicism is more than a system of beliefs; it is a way of being that brings us into union with Jesus Christ. Catholicism is a far more effective means of reaching Christ than any effort we could make on our own because Christ Himself established the Church as the way to Himself: He set the teachings, the laws, the sacraments, and the actions we need to follow and perform to draw close to Him. The goal in life is to enter into union with God. We are much better served if we follow the way to union given to us by God's Son than adhering to any way we devise on our own.

45. AREN'T ALL RELIGIONS BASICALLY THE SAME?

No. As noted in the prior question, religion is a human way of relating to the supernatural. Culture, time, people, and place all contribute to differences among religions, but how the practitioners of a particular religion perceive God is the decisive difference.

For example, Catholics believe that Jesus is God, so we follow His teachings and commandments. This fact distinguishes Catholicism from Judaism, which, though it professes belief in the same God, is very different in its teachings and its adherents' practices because it does not acknowledge Jesus as the Savior of the World.

A religion's effectiveness hinges upon how closely it attains to the truth about God. Religions also need to attain to objective truth concerning good and evil. A religion that contradicts objective truth or the moral law, for example, by commanding human sacrifice or by sanctioning adultery, is a false religion. Satanic cults and other groups that seek to conjure evil are not religions, even if they call themselves such. A religion, properly speaking, seeks the divine; it does not seek evil.

Since religions seek after the one God, there will be overlap between them insofar as they identify certain truths about Him and about human beings. Judaism, for example, teaches the truths of the one God and His commandments, but it falls short in failing to recognize Christ. Islam is correct that there is one God, but it misrepresents who this God is. Other religions that do not recognize the one God are gravely deficient, but they may overlap with Catholicism if they propose moral teachings that resemble the Ten Commandments.

Catholicism contains the fullness of the truth about God and about how to grow closer to Him. Various Christian denominations hold many of the same truths that Catholicism teaches, but in rejecting some of those truths, they lack the complete means that God has revealed to us. As the Second Vatican Council's *Nostra Aetate* teaches,

> The Catholic Church rejects nothing that is true and holy in these religions. She regards with sincere reverence those ways of conduct and of life, those precepts and teachings which, though differing in many aspects from the ones she holds and sets forth, nonetheless often reflect a ray of that Truth which enlightens all men. Indeed, she proclaims, and ever must proclaim Christ "the way, the truth, and the life" (John 14:6), in whom men may find the fullness of religious life, in whom God has reconciled all things to Himself.[3]

---

[3] Declaration on the Relation of the Church to Non-Christian Religions, *Nostra Aetate*, 2.

46. DO CATHOLICS, JEWS, AND MUSLIMS BELIEVE IN THE SAME GOD?

Catholics and Jews certainly worship the same God. Jews see God as our loving Father, but they do not see Him in His fullness: as a Trinity of Persons, Father, Son, and Holy Spirit. Analogously, they see the half-moon, but not the full moon. Muslims worship one God, but whether Catholics and Muslims worship the same God is contested; some affirm this while others deny it. Based on the Quran's description of God, it is more likely that they believe in a different God than Catholics, who, unlike Muslims, affirm that God is love as three Persons in one God.

47. WHY IS CATHOLICISM THE TRUE RELIGION?

No independent tests or criteria exist by which we can evaluate religions in an objective manner. Instead, we can consider each one on its own terms, and under the leadership of each one's best practitioners (that is, by its saints, not its sinners) in light of the goal that each professes to reach. Though most religions primarily focus on the divine, many have a derivative component: the promotion of human flourishing. In view of that, Catholicism is the true religion because it best protects, nourishes, and develops the human being in relation to God. We can substantiate this claim by looking at Catholicism under three facets that are common to all religions: what it is, what it commands, and what it promises.

Catholicism is a religion of redemption: God comes to us to rescue us from our sufferings and our sins because we cannot rescue ourselves. In sacrificing Himself for us, Jesus Christ shows us how to live and reiterates that lesson with one all-encompassing commandment: love one another as I have loved you. In loving God and loving our neighbor, we find joy in God, the promise of Catholicism.

Of all religions, Catholicism portrays an image of the human person that is the most beautiful while at the same time not ignoring the inevitability of suffering. Its doctrine, laws, and promises meet us where we are, prevent us from exacerbating our sufferings and sins, and bring us to God, the ultimate end of our existence, not via Easy Street—a route foreign to human nature—but via Calvary. In the Cross, we find redemption, and with it the truth of our humanity.

Catholicism is the true religion. The powerful words of the Second Vatican Council's *Gaudium et Spes* summarize this approach of assessing religions in light of what they do for human beings: Jesus Christ, "by the revelation of the mystery of the Father and His love, fully reveals man to man himself and makes his supreme calling clear."[4]

48. WHAT'S THE DIFFERENCE BETWEEN BEING SPIRITUAL AND BEING RELIGIOUS?

Taking the words by their definitions, a person is *spiritual* if he lives conscious of his soul and of his connection to God; a person is *religious* if he exercises his soul and relationship with God through an established way of worship, belief, and morals. As such, being spiritual and being religious are not mutually exclusive; they overlap considerably. Yet when the terms are used today, they are bifurcated; it is implied that the spiritual person relates to God on his own terms while the religious person relates to God through an organized religion.

[4]   Vatican Council II, Pastoral Constitution on the Church in the Modern World *Gaudium et Spes* (December 7, 1965), no. 22.

The bifurcation of the terms *spiritual* and *religious* is the product of a radically individualistic world that prizes the individual's freedom from all constraints — religious, familial, societal, and biological — so that each person can seemingly create himself anew with every decision he makes. This perspective is contrary to human nature, which is inherently dependent on biology, family, and society to live in a healthy and happy manner.

Religion, too, is grounded in human nature: we are hardwired to worship things higher than ourselves, and we do so best in community and through forms received from our ancestors whose wisdom teaches us and whose sins warn us. No one human being has all the answers; it is foolish for an individual to believe he can find his way to God on his own. It is far more effective to relate to God through established forms, especially since, for Catholics, these forms — the sacraments, the teachings of the Church, the moral law — come directly from God and therefore lead back to Him.

49. *DO CATHOLICS HAVE TO BELIEVE ALL THE CHURCH'S TEACHINGS?*

Yes. The Church is the custodian of Christ's own teachings, so it follows that to believe the Church's teachings is to believe Christ's. The bedrock of Church teaching, called the *deposit of faith*, is what God has revealed in the Old Testament and in the New Testament in Christ. We recite a succinct summary of this revelation each Sunday at Mass in the Nicene Creed.

There is more to God's revelation, and therefore to the deposit of faith, than what is contained in the Creed: the necessity of the Church and the sacraments, the special privileges of the Blessed Virgin Mary, the roles of the pope and the bishops, the mission of the lay faithful, and more. To believe in Christ and to be a member of the Church includes believing in all these teachings as well because they come from God, even as the Church has developed a more definitive articulation of them over time.

God also revealed how we are to live in union with Him, so the Church's moral teachings come from God as well. These include the Beatitudes and the Ten Commandments, whose teachings on marriage and on relationships with other people Christ made more demanding. To believe the Church's teachings on the moral life is to believe God Himself. Or, to express it another way, to be a Christian is to follow all the teachings of Christ that comprise the deposit of faith.

Given that the Church's teachings on matters of faith and of morals come directly from God, Catholics should *want* to believe all these teachings and live them to the full. Sadly, the world today loudly preaches a very different faith and urges a moral life contrary to the one that God revealed. We are always better served following God and the Church than following the prevailing ideas of a secular culture that has rejected God.

50. *I HAVE DOUBTS. IS SOMETHING WRONG WITH ME?*

No. One of the great challenges of faith is that we cannot see the God whom we love. By its nature, then, faith can generate spiritual unrest, for it reaches for God but cannot touch Him. It is normal, then, to encounter difficulties concerning belief in God and in His Church's teachings.

When it comes to faith, our contemporary world uses *difficulty* and *doubt* as synonyms, but they are not. A difficulty is a roadblock or hardship that can weaken a person's faith that generally arises from uncertain knowledge. For example, a person may say, "I have difficulty understanding how Jesus can be fully God and fully man at the same time," or "I do not understand why the Church teaches that IVF is immoral." Many Catholics have such questions, and wrestling with them is a regular part of the life of faith.

A doubt, by contrast, is the willful withholding of belief in something, as, for example, a child would say, "I doubt that the moon is made of cheese." Catholics who practice their Faith and desire to be in relationship with God experience difficulties, not doubts. Their difficulties are a normal part of the spiritual life. They call us to find answers in order to grow deeper in our faith. As St. John Henry Newman famously said, "Ten thousand difficulties do not make one doubt."

CHAPTER 8

WHAT JESUS CHRIST MEANS
FOR THE WORLD – AND FOR ME

†

51. HOW DO WE KNOW JESUS REALLY EXISTED?

Beyond a shadow of a doubt, Jesus of Nazareth, whom believers call Jesus Christ, meaning "Jesus the Anointed One of God," was a real man who was born during the reign of the Roman Emperor Augustus (31 B.C. — A.D. 14) and died, after a few years of public ministry in what is now modern Israel, during the reign of the emperor Tiberius (A.D. 14 — 37).

Jesus' existence is well attested not only by the Gospels and other New Testament documents, but also by pagan and Jewish writers of the ancient world. There is as much evidence for Jesus' existence as for many other famous figures of antiquity, including Socrates, Plato, Aristotle, Alexander the Great, Cicero, and Caesar. The fact of Jesus' existence is certain. The proper question is not whether Jesus existed, but whether He is God.

52. JESUS LIVED TWO THOUSAND YEARS AGO – HOW CAN HE SAVE ALL PEOPLE THROUGH HISTORY?

This is the most startling claim of Christianity: that one man who lived two thousand years ago is the Savior of all people who ever lived and who will ever live. This is only possible because Jesus is God. His deeds, which happened at a particular moment in time, speak of His divine power, which transcends the limits of time and space. Christ's death and Resurrection, the culmination of God's action in the world, reverberate into the past, present, and future.

Jesus is not just a man who lived two thousand years ago. He is the God-Man who alone makes a claim over all human beings who have ever lived. To make His saving sacrifice present to every moment in time, Christ established the Mass, which is the unbloody re-presentation of His Crucifixion, and commanded that we do it in remembrance of Him. Every time we attend Mass, the singular event of Christ's saving death is brought to us in the present moment.

53. HOW CAN JESUS BE BOTH GOD AND MAN?

First, since we know Jesus is a real man, we must identify how we know He is God before we can speak of how He is both God and man. Jesus' identity and mission are linked: He is the Christ, the Savior, because He is God; He could not save us if He were not God. Therefore, proving His divinity to us was a foundational element of His public ministry. He did this in two ways: through His unprecedented teachings and through His miracles.

Concerning His teachings, both the style and the content of Jesus' teachings were utterly unique within the Jewish tradition. In the Sermon on the Mount, when He declared repeatedly, "You have heard that it was said . . . but I say to you," He was asserting an authority greater than Moses, the chief prophet and lawgiver of the Jewish people. He did so while sitting down rather than standing up, another claim of authority.

When He declared, "Amen, Amen, I say to you," He was demanding belief in what He was about to say. When, at the conclusion of the Beatitudes, He promised, "Blessed are you when men revile you and persecute you and utter all kinds of evil against you falsely *on my account*," (Matt 5:11), He claimed an authority greater than the prophets. He announced that He was greater than the Sabbath, the essential day of worship for the Jews, and greater than the Temple, the solemn center of worship. And what He taught was hitherto unimaginable: that divorce is wrong, that we must love our enemies as ourselves, that we should submit to persecution, that we should leave behind everything and follow Him. Jesus' listeners noticed the difference: "The crowds were astonished at His teaching, for he taught them as one who had authority, and not as their scribes" (Matt. 7:28–29).

What kind of a person could teach these lessons in this manner? As C. S. Lewis famously wrote, based on the evidence, Jesus is either a lunatic, a liar, or the Lord. Given the rationality with which Jesus spoke, He was not a lunatic; given the fact that He willingly accepted His death, He could not have been a liar. Therefore, He can only be the Lord.

Regarding miracles, Jesus explained at the Last Supper that He performed mighty works to reassure our belief in Him. "Believe me that I am in the Father and the Father in me; or else believe me for the sake of the works themselves" (John 14:11). Of His own power He could not have performed these miracles — healing the sick, driving out demons, walking on water, calming storms, multiplying loaves of bread, raising the dead — unless He were God.

In Himself, Jesus is God who chose to take on human flesh and enter the world as any other man: He was born of a woman. We call this the *Incarnation*, which literally means "made into flesh." Jesus is truly God, therefore, but He is also truly man. He assumed every aspect of human nature: flesh, will, mind, and soul. The only way He does not resemble us is that He did not sin. In this way, Jesus has a more complete human existence than we do, for He always uses His freedom correctly to choose the good. Sin, by contrast, dehumanizes us, for through sin we fall short of what we were made to be. Hence, we refer to Jesus as the "God-Man" because He is both God and man. He is unique among all beings: He is one Divine Person who possesses not one but two natures: a divine nature and a human nature. The two natures are perfectly united in His Person, in the words of the Council of Chalcedon in 451, "without confusion or change, without division or separation."

54. WHAT DOES IT MEAN TO SAY JESUS IS THE "SON OF GOD"?

Jesus, as noted in the prior question, is God. To call Him the "Son of God" refers to His personhood as God, who is one being yet three Persons: Father, Son, and Holy Spirit. Each Person of the Trinity equally possesses the one divine nature; their differences come from their eternal relationships to one another.

The Father is the first principle of origin within God (though not in the sense of being *before* the Son and the Holy Spirit); the Son is the Father's perfect expression of Himself; the Holy Spirit is the personified love that overflows from the Father and the Son.

The Preface to the Most Holy Trinity, recited at Mass before the Eucharistic Prayer, captures the essence of the Trinity and the relationship of the three Persons as well as limited human language can:

> It is truly right and just, our duty and our salvation, always and everywhere to give you thanks, Lord, holy Father, almighty and eternal God. For with your Only Begotten Son and the Holy Spirit you are one God,

one Lord: not in the unity of a single person, but in a Trinity of one substance. For what you have revealed to us of your glory we believe equally of your Son and of the Holy Spirit, so that, in the confessing of the true and eternal Godhead, you might be adored in what is proper to each Person, their unity in substance, and their equality in majesty.[5]

In the Incarnation, the Son, the second Person of the Trinity, entered time as man. His union with human nature is permanent, even now as He reigns in Heaven. St. Irenaeus of Lyons (ca. 130–202) famously captured the mystery of Jesus' mission within the Trinity: "The Son of God became the Son of Man so that we, sons of men, could become sons of God."

55. HOW DO WE KNOW THE RESURRECTION OF CHRIST FROM THE DEAD IS REAL?

St. Paul communicates the ultimatum: "If Christ has not been raised, then our preaching is in vain and your faith is in vain" (1 Cor. 15:14). The Resurrection of Jesus is the ultimate manifestation of His divinity and the veracity of His teachings. As with Jesus' miracles (Q64), the evidence for the reality of the Resurrection is overwhelming.

First, Jesus' own followers proclaimed Jesus' Resurrection just three days after He died. By contrast, myths and made-up stories about heroes take time to develop. St. Paul's first letters proclaiming Jesus' Resurrection were written within two decades of the

---

[5]   *The Roman Missal,* Third Typical Edition. Page 1328.

Resurrection, and the Gospel accounts followed shortly thereafter. Paul and the evangelists recorded what they had seen and heard, either directly for themselves or from witnesses, and these accounts began with the event itself.

Second, the Gospel narratives consistently describe the risen Jesus, whose newly glorified body defies all previous myths and stories. He is the same person, yet transformed; He can walk through doors, yet He can be touched and He can eat; He can appear and disappear at will, yet He is not a ghost. The consistency of Jesus' portrayal across the Gospels is only possible because the evangelists are describing true events.

Third, on Good Friday the disciples were dejected and scattered. Three days later, they suddenly were overjoyed and confident in the face of opposition. For their behavior to have changed so quickly and starkly, something astonishing must have happened to them.

Fourth, following from the previous point, ten of the eleven apostles who claimed to have seen Jesus risen from the dead were violently killed for professing this — not one recanted under the threat of torture and excruciating death. If Jesus had not risen, why would they surrender their lives for belief in that fact?

Fifth, Saul of Tarsus was a fearsome persecutor of the first Christians, even consenting to kill them. Overnight, he became an apostle who traveled the world for the risen Jesus, eventually enduring martyrdom himself. For such a transformation to have occurred, Paul, as he became after Baptism, had to have been utterly convinced of what he had seen.

Sixth, Jesus' Resurrection was proclaimed in the very city where He was buried. If the tomb had not been empty, this proclamation would have been refuted instantly. Moreover, Jesus' enemies admitted the tomb was empty; they claimed, to distract from this fact, that His disciples had stolen His body (Matt. 28:13–15).

Seventh, the first witnesses of the empty tomb and claimants to have seen the risen Jesus were women, whose testimony was not considered valid. If the disciples were making up the story of the Resurrection, they would not have based it on women's testimony.

Eighth, belief in the risen Jesus spread quickly in Jerusalem and then abroad. Before long, Jews who believed shifted their Sabbath observance — the very core of Jewish identity — from Saturday to Sunday. For people to change their lives so dramatically, they had to be convinced that Christ really rose.

Finally, counter-arguments that try to discredit the Resurrection all fall short. To claim it was a hoax, a myth, or the disciples' hallucination fails to account for all the evidence described above. It requires far more faith to believe that Jesus did not rise from the dead than to believe that He did.

56. IF CHRIST'S DEATH DEFEATED SIN, WHY IS THERE STILL EVIL?

With Christ's death, sin and Satan have been vanquished; God's love has triumphed. Yet the war against sin continues. As we saw in the parable of the weeds among the wheat (Matt. 13:24–30) (Q23), God still wants us to fight against sin before completely ending the contest at the end of time. Fighting against evil, sin, and Satan is one way we show our love of God. This includes opposing evil in society and the temptations we feel regularly within ourselves. It is at the end of time that evil and sin will finally be no more.

57. COULD THERE BE ANOTHER MESSIAH COMING?

No. Jesus is the final revelation of God. He alone is the Messiah, the Christ, God's anointed one. God spent all of history preparing us for Jesus; that is the record of the Old Testament. Since the coming of the Holy Spirit at Pentecost, human beings have been tasked with living and spreading Jesus' teaching. That is our project until the end of time.

58. WHAT DOES IT MEAN THAT JESUS WILL COME AGAIN?

At the end of time there will be a Final Judgment, when God brings all the good who have ever existed to Himself and banishes all evildoers forever from His presence. Jesus will come again to earth triumphantly; we call this the *Parousia*, which will inaugurate the Final Judgment, as we proclaim in the Nicene Creed each Sunday: "He will come again in glory to judge the living and the dead."

Each year the Church prepares us for the Parousia on the First Sunday of Advent, which means "arrival." As with the Final Judgment, the Parousia is an event of joy and fear: joy at the coming of our God who gave His life for us, fear at the reality of our sins that make us unworthy of Him.

CHAPTER 9

THE BIBLE AND ITS
INTERPRETATION

†

59. WHAT IS THE BIBLE? WHERE DID IT COME FROM AND HOW DO WE KNOW IT ISN'T MADE UP?

The Bible, with its forty-six books of the Old Testament and twenty-seven books of the New Testament, is the written record of God's revelation of Himself to human beings in history. For that reason, each of the books within the Bible has been cherished for centuries by ancient Israel (Old Testament) and by the Church (Old and New Testaments).

Within the Church, the books of the Bible have been incorporated into the celebration of the Mass since the beginning. The Church has passed these books on continuously from one generation to the next to the present day. As the Bible's custodian for so many centuries, the Church recognizes and guarantees its authenticity: the seventy-three books that we have are God's Word.

60. WHY DO WE NEED THE CHURCH TO HELP US INTERPRET THE BIBLE?

The Bible did not fall from the sky like a meteor containing a code. It is the written record of God's revelation to the Church, as recorded by members of the Church. The Church, as the recipient of God's inspired Word, is also its authoritative interpreter according to Jesus, who gave the apostles, and, in turn, their successors the bishops, the authority to make binding decisions that represent God's will (Matt. 18:18–19; John 16:13).

St. John Henry Newman converted to Catholicism from Anglicanism when he realized that the Church is necessary to safeguard, protect, and interpret the Bible. Without the Church's divinely established authority, there is no way to resolve disputes over the meaning of the Bible. Hence Newman wrote in his *Essay on the Development of Christian Doctrine* that it is "common sense" that "some authority there must be if there is a revelation given, and other authority there is none" except the Church.[6]

When the meaning of certain verses or passages is in dispute, the Church, by the power of the Holy Spirit, gives them official interpretations which are called *dogmas*. It is important to note that most of the Bible has not received official interpretations. Catholics are free, therefore, to interpret the Bible within the bounds of the deposit of faith, that is, within the parameters of the Church's perennial teachings. They may do so more profitably, however, with the guidance of the Church Fathers and theologians carefully attuned to the Bible's spiritual meaning.

61. SHOULD I READ THE BIBLE HISTORICALLY OR FOR A LESSON?

The most important takeaway from reading the Bible is to understand what God is communicating to us spiritually. He speaks to the whole Church as well as to each of us as individuals. The spiritual reading of the Bible, therefore, takes priority. But we cannot arrive at this

---

6   John Henry Cardinal Newman, *An Essay on the Development of Christian Doctrine*, 10th ed. (London: Longmans, Green, 1897), 88.

spiritual reading apart from the historical and literary aspects of the Bible. The historical context and literary style of each of the seventy-three books are the means through which God speaks to us. Knowing each enables us to reach sharper insights into how God was acting in history and how He invites us today into relationship with Him.

For example, the Creation stories (Gen. 1–2) are poetic stories of how God created the heavens and earth. They are neither newspaper-like nor scientific accounts that relate specific happenings. They communicate what God wants us to know about Himself and how He is the author of all that is. Each detail in the Creation stories teaches different lessons about God, His majesty, and His intentions for creation. Each lesson about God in these chapters is true.

The Creation stories do not rival science. On one level, the Creation stories and science are complementary: the Bible tells us how and why the world exists and science tells us what the world is, materially speaking. In other words, the Bible and science seek to explain different things: the former explains essences and the latter measures demonstrable things. Yet, on another level, science is subservient to creation — science could not exist if God did not create the world and order it as He did. Science operates within the sphere established by God and articulated in the biblical Creation stories.

62. ARE THE STORIES IN THE OLD TESTAMENT TO BE INTERPRETED LITERALLY?

In general, the entirety of the Old Testament must be interpreted in light of its fulfillment in Jesus Christ. The varying messages and stories within it all point to Him. In many instances, what was written in the Old Testament remained obscure until the coming of Christ. For example, Isaiah's prophecy to King Ahaz in the eighth century B.C. — "Behold, a young woman [virgin] shall conceive and bear a son, and shall call his name Immanuel" (Isa. 7:14) — was a mystery until Christ was born of the Blessed Virgin Mary.

The Old Testament's forty-six books were written in many different styles and literary genres. The truth and the interpretation of these books depend largely on their literary genre — history, epic poetry, psalms, wisdom literature, and prophetic writings each have their unique ways of expressing God's message to us and are to be interpreted accordingly. For example, the story of Jonah, who was swallowed by a fish and remained in its belly for three days and three nights, is not history in the strict sense; it is a prophecy, and, as such, communicates certain truths about God's mercy and the need for human beings to repent of their sins. In this way, all the biblical stories are true insofar as they communicate God's perspective. Admittedly, however, in a few instances what exactly God is revealing can be challenging to discern. When this happens, we know in faith that the answer to these mysteries lies within the deposit of faith.

63. WHY IS GOD PORTRAYED SO DIFFERENTLY IN THE OLD AND NEW TESTAMENTS?

In both the Old and the New Testaments, God condemns sin and offers His mercy. The difference between the two testaments is not God — if it were, then He would not be God, but a shape-shifting transformer. Rather, the difference is how the one God approaches us: in the Old Testament, God conceals His face from us because of the sins we committed; in the New Testament, God reveals His face in Jesus Christ, who comes to forgive our sins. The New Testament, then, is the witness of God's new tactics toward us — tactics that fulfill what the Old Testament had prepared yet concealed.

In Christ, God inaugurates the New and Eternal Covenant that extends beyond Israel to all nations. It is a covenant of love and mercy, for sure, but woe to him who rejects His mercy: "He who believes in the Son has eternal life; he who does not obey the Son shall not see life, but the wrath of God rests upon him" (John 3:36).

St. Augustine famously wrote that the New Testament lies hidden in the Old and the Old is revealed in the New. God may have waited to reveal His face but He has revealed the same message from the time of Abraham through our own day. That message is clear: receive God's love, freely offered, but woe to him who rejects it.

64. HOW DO WE KNOW JESUS PERFORMED MIRACLES? COULD THE DISCIPLES HAVE MADE THEM UP?

The evidence for Jesus' miracles is overwhelming. It is far more plausible, based on the evidence, to believe that Jesus' miracles occurred than that they were made up. The following factors testify to the veracity of Jesus' miracles as recorded in the Gospels:

First, every level of the Gospel tradition reports that Jesus performed miracles. Even His enemies acknowledged them; they tried to discredit them rather than deny them by claiming that it is "by Beelzebul, the prince of demons, that this man casts out demons" (Matt. 12:24). The Jewish nonbeliever Josephus, writing in the late first century A.D., called Jesus a miracle worker. Multiple sources reporting the same thing are difficult to repudiate.

Second, the reactions of the miracles' witnesses testify that they really saw wondrous things. For example, when Jesus multiplied the loaves to feed the crowd, they sought to make Him king (John

6:14–15). If He had merely been telling stories and teaching, the crowd would not have reacted with such conviction.

Third, small details included within descriptions of the miracles point to their veracity. For example, why would the Gospel writers, who were writing in Greek, incorporate Aramaic words within their accounts? Because Jesus spoke Aramaic, and the astonished witnesses of the miracles reported the event as they experienced it, using Jesus' own words that spurred the action. He declared *Talitha koum* when he raised the daughter of Jairus (Mark 5:41) and *Ephphatha* when he healed a deaf man (Mark 7:34). The only reason to include these words is that Jesus actually said them at the moments described.

Fourth, Jesus' miracles transcend the limits of nature but do not contradict nature — He never took dirt from the ground and molded it into a bird. Such actions would beggar belief. Jesus' miracles correspond perfectly with His ministry: He came to heal us of our sin and feed our souls spiritually; His miracles healed and fed His disciples physically.

Fifth, we cannot reject Jesus' miracles on the grounds that they are unprecedented or because we think they could not happen. The former denies history, and the latter is an act of faith in our own intellectual powers.

If God is God, He has the power to intervene in the universe He created; a person is wrong to assume the contrary. As God, Jesus can also intervene in the universe. To deny this is to deny a preponderance of evidence.

CHAPTER 10

THE CHURCH AND THE
SACRAMENTS

†

65. WHAT IS THE PURPOSE OF THE CHURCH? CAN'T I MEET GOD ON MY OWN?

When God first revealed Himself to Abraham, He made clear that He was calling a particular people to Himself: Israel. Christ reconstituted this people, opening membership to anyone who would believe in Him. This reconstituted people is the Church, and it grows directly from Israel, whose twelve tribes foreshadowed the creation of twelve apostles who would lead the Church after Christ ascended to His Father in Heaven. In other words, God planted the seeds for the Church deep in the past, and the seeds flowered into the Church on the feast of Pentecost.

The Church is God's people, an assembly of believers intimately connected to Christ, who is the Church's head. The Church, then, extends Christ's Incarnation into time so that those who did not see Him walking on earth can meet Him and receive His grace directly. Christ willed the sacraments as the chief means by which He communicates His grace, that is, His divine power, for the sacraments are incarnational: they make invisible grace perceptible through physical signs. As the jewel in the crown, Christ instituted the Eucharist, His own Body and Blood, which we can only receive through the Church, to whom He entrusted it.

The Church is not a stodgy organization that seeks to control individuals. She is rather a dynamic gathering of people on pilgrimage to meet God the Father through God the Son animated by God the Holy Spirit. In the words of historian Christopher Dawson, the Church "is the bearer of a living tradition which unites the present and the past, the living and the dead, in one great spiritual community which transcends all the limited communities of race and nation and state."[7] To help us on the way, the Church offers us Christ's teachings, sacraments, and laws, and she does so under the leadership of the pope and bishops, whom Christ willed to succeed the apostles as governors of the Church. Every aspect of the Church's life serves a single end: leading her people to God.

Without the Church, we are separated from the Body of Christ. Without the Church, it is infinitely more difficult to relate to God. Without the Church, we are cut off from the life-giving sacraments that communicate Christ's grace directly to us. If we try to relate to God on our own, we are far more likely to find a caricature of God, one made in our own image and likeness, than the real God who created Heaven and earth.

66. WHY DOES THE CHURCH HAVE SO MANY TEACHINGS – CAN THEY CHANGE?

The many teachings of the Church exist because they all emanate from a single source that is infinite in mystery and majesty: the triune God who is Father, Son, and Holy Spirit. It is because there is so much to learn about Him and so many consequences that stem from Him

---

[7]   Christopher Dawson, *The Kingdom of God and History*, "Christianity and European Culture," ed. Gerald J. Russello (Washington, D.C.: The Catholic University of America Press, 1998), 210.

that the Church has so many teachings. The key point is to recall the unity of these teachings in God as, to continue the analogy from the introduction, all the branches and leaves of a tree are connected to a single trunk.

The teachings of the Church that concern faith and morals cannot change precisely because they come from God whose revelation is definitive and without error. The Church does offer other teachings that are directed toward temporal rather than eternal ends, such as the relationship between Church and State, the moral dimension of the economy, and how to deal with emerging technologies. Since these teachings are not revealed by God, they can change over time.

Sadly, this idea of teachings developing over time is largely lost on our modern secular culture, which perceives all rules and teachings as restrictive of individual freedom. This perspective is exactly opposite of how Catholic doctrine should be perceived. The firmness of Catholic doctrine provides solid ground on which we can build our lives; we know this ground will always be stable no matter how stormy the weather above it grows. We are free to build our homes on this ground as we wish, provided we do not violate the ground's integrity. The same goes for living according to the teachings of the Church: an infinitude of ways to live exists within the parameters of Christ's teachings. The Church adds that living outside those parameters in sin, despite the seeming allure, brings only sadness and destruction; Christ offered the parable of the prodigal son (Luke 15:11–32) to warn us of this reality.

Therefore, we ought to give thanks that Catholic doctrine is so stable because it guarantees the integrity of our lives.

67. *WHAT IS THE PURPOSE OF THE SACRAMENTS?*

The sacraments are the means Christ established to communicate to us His grace, His divine power that saves us from sin and transforms us, slowly, into saints who live permanently in God's love.

The sacraments all work in the same manner. Because we are physical beings who, like the apostle Thomas after the Resurrection, long to touch what we believe, the sacraments are physical or verbal signs, either material (bread, wine, water, oil) or spoken (the contrition of a believer confessing sins, the consent of spouses to marry) through which, when the Church offers the appropriate prayers, God sends His grace. In other words, the sign is the vessel or channel of God, who touches us directly through them.

Sacraments are necessary for our salvation because they are the primary means by which God communicates His saving grace to us. All seven sacraments — Baptism, Confirmation, Eucharist, Penance, Anointing of the Sick, Matrimony, Holy Orders — were established by Christ and entrusted to the Church to administer and preserve. Each gives us a specific grace to live holier lives: Baptism removes sin, fills us with the Holy Spirit, and adopts us as God's children forever; Confirmation strengths us to live our Faith in a hostile world; Penance brings the forgiveness of sins after we confess them; Anointing of the Sick strengthens our souls to battle illness and death; Matrimony and Holy Orders are ways to serve God through serving others over the long course of our lives. And then there is the greatest sacrament: the Holy Eucharist, in which Christ Himself becomes food to nourish our souls; to receive Christ in Holy Communion is the closest we can get to God this side of Heaven.

Hence sacraments are tremendous gifts that we should seek eagerly because they put us in direct contact with God Himself. Sadly, like gifts of family and friends, we too often take the sacramental gifts for granted and forget their awesome power. To receive a sacrament is to be touched personally by Christ. For such a privilege we should thank God daily.

68. WHAT HAPPENS AT BAPTISM? WHAT IF A BABY DOESN'T GET BAPTIZED?

Without question, Baptism is the most important — and most under-appreciated — event in a person's life. When a person is baptized, he is adopted as a child of God forever. To be God's son or God's daughter is an incredible gift, for through this adoption human beings are invited to live in communion with Him in His family forever and to receive all the blessings He offers us through His Church. Hence Baptism is often described as a door, for as the water is poured onto his head, the recipient enters a new life with God that would not be possible without this sacrament.

In addition to incorporating the recipient into God's family forever, Baptism serves another function: It cleanses the person being baptized of every kind of sin, including Original Sin, which is the state of deprivation of God's grace into which all human beings are born. Through Baptism, even infants who have not committed personal sin are removed from this state of deprivation and brought into union with God.

We do not know what happens to a baby who dies before being baptized. The *Catechism* teaches that "the Church can only entrust [deceased infants] to the mercy of God," which "allow[s] us to hope that there is a way of salvation for children who have died without Baptism" (*CCC* 1261).

It has become fashionable in certain circles for parents to put off a child's Baptism until he or she is older and can make a personal decision. This is a colossal mistake. To deprive a child of Baptism is akin to depriving him of an education or health care. Parents would never make teeth brushing, handwashing, or school optional for their children. Likewise, they should never make God and His grace optional. God is essential and Baptism is the means by which human beings begin to encounter God in His fullness.

69. WHAT IS THE EUCHARIST?

The Eucharist is an astonishing miracle: ordinary bread and wine, at the command of a priest repeating the words of our Savior, are transformed into the Body and Blood of Jesus Christ. The bread and wine remain visible but they are no longer present. It is Christ's Body and Christ's Blood that are present under the appearances of bread and wine.

The only way that the Eucharist can be Christ's Body and Blood is by His power. And the only way we know this is because He commanded us at the Last Supper to repeat what He did — take and eat His Body under the appearance of bread, take and drink His Blood under the appearance of wine — "Do this in memory of me." Without that command, the Eucharist would be impossible.

Because the Eucharist is Christ Himself, the Church rightly calls it "the source and summit of the whole Christian life" (CCC 1324). As Christ Himself, the Eucharist is our reason for living or the summit we are trying to reach; for the same reason, the Eucharist is the source of divine grace that helps us live according to God's will. As such, the Eucharist is the center of our worship — it is the Mass's greatest fruit — and the greatest means to our sanctification. As St. Carlo Acutis put it, "The Eucharist is our highway to Heaven."

As noted earlier (Q55), St. Paul wrote that if Christ is not risen, our faith is in vain. In a similar manner, we can say that if the Eucharist is not really Christ, then our religion that has made the Eucharist its center is a farce. But we know for sure that the Eucharist is Christ because Christ Himself said so. As St. Thomas Aquinas wrote in his hymn "Adoro te devote," "I believe whatever the Son of God has said. Nothing is truer than His word of truth."

70. CAN DIVORCED PEOPLE RECEIVE COMMUNION?

God hates divorce (see Mal. 2:15–16). Divorce contradicts the order of marriage that God created to last until the death of the spouses. Christ emphatically forbade divorce when the Pharisees tried to justify it: "Have you not read that He who made them from the beginning made them male and female, and said, 'For this reason a man shall leave his father and mother and be joined to his wife, and the two shall become one'? So they are no longer two but one. What therefore God has joined together, let not man put asunder.... For the hardness of your heart Moses allowed you to divorce your wives, but from the beginning it was not so" (Matt. 19:4–6, 8).

Though divorce is a sin, the culpability of the husband and wife in a divorce varies according to the circumstances — and, depending on those circumstances, may be grounds for a decree of nullity (annulment), a determination by the proper ecclesial authorities that no sacramental marriage took place.

It is possible for one spouse to be without guilt in a situation that leads to divorce, as would be the case, for example, if the wife were a victim of abuse. In such instances, to abide by the commandment of Christ, the Church counsels separation to protect the wife but not divorce. Without question this is a situation of great suffering that can be healed only by uniting it in prayer with Christ on the Cross.

Catholics who are civilly divorced but have not had their marriage declared null by the Church are still married in the eyes of God. Therefore, if a Catholic in this situation remarries civilly, he is entering into an adulterous union. He cannot receive Holy Communion in this state since he is living in a state of mortal sin that puts him at odds with Christ whom he would be receiving. By contrast, Catholics who are divorced but not remarried may receive Holy Communion, which is often a great source of consolation for them.

71. WHY DO I HAVE TO GO TO MASS?

First, we go to Mass because of what it is: the Mass is the unbloody re-presentation of Christ's saving sacrifice on the Cross on Good Friday. Christ's Crucifixion is the definitive event that saved the world. Because of this fact, it cannot remain confined to the past — it must be made present every day, and it is made present each time the Mass is celebrated anywhere in the world.

Second, we go to Mass because of what it does for us: It brings us into union with Christ in His glory so we can be transformed from sinners to saints. To worship God and to subordinate our wills to His make us better people; the grace of Christ's sacrifice gives us the power to do this. We receive that grace from praying diligently at Mass, but then in a deeper way when we receive the fruit of the Mass — the Eucharist — in Holy Communion.

Going to Mass allows us to unite with Jesus Himself — this is the closest we can come to God this side of eternity. Receiving the

Eucharist at Mass is the path to salvation, as Jesus Himself said: "I am the living bread which came down from heaven; if any one eats of this bread, he will live for ever; and the bread which I shall give for the life of the world is my flesh" (John 6:51).

Third, we go to Mass because Christ's sacrifice, in reconciling sinful human beings with God, is the ultimate act of worship of God. Human beings are hardwired by nature to worship something. The question is what. In his famous 2005 commencement speech at Kenyon College, professor and novelist David Foster Wallace, who was not a Christian, starkly expressed the human tendency to worship:

> In the day to day trenches of adult life, there is actually no such thing as atheism. There is no such thing as not worshipping. Everybody worships. The only choice we get is what to worship. And the compelling reason for maybe choosing some sort of God or spiritual-type thing to worship ... is that pretty much anything else you worship will eat you alive. If you worship money and things, if they are where you tap real meaning in life, then you will never have enough, never feel you have enough. It's the truth. Worship your body and beauty and sexual allure and you will always feel ugly. And when time and age start showing, you will die a million deaths before they finally grieve you....
>
> Worship power, you will end up feeling weak and afraid, and you will need ever more power over others to numb you to your own fear. Worship your intellect, being seen as smart, you will end up feeling stupid, a fraud, always on the verge of being found out. But the insidious thing about these forms of worship is not

that they're evil or sinful, it's that they're unconscious. They are default settings.

They're the kind of worship you just gradually slip into, day after day, getting more and more selective about what you see and how you measure value without ever being fully aware that that's what you're doing.

And the so-called real world will not discourage you from operating on your default settings, because the so-called real world of men and money and power hums merrily along in a pool of fear and anger and frustration and craving and worship of self.[8]

Catholics know that worshipping God frees us from all these false gods mentioned by Wallace that can ensnare us in our own egos. When we choose to worship God, worldly things, rather than control our lives, take their proper place in our lives. And the greatest way to worship God is to join our hearts and minds with the sacrifice of Christ as it is being re-presented in the Mass, for there we find our salvation from our selfishness and sins.

72. WHY CAN'T WOMEN BE PRIESTS?

Ordaining women to the priesthood is impossible for three reasons. First, when a priest celebrates Mass, he is acting in the Person of Jesus Christ. During the Mass, when the priest says, "This is My Body ... This is the chalice of My Blood," he is not speaking of his own body, but Christ's Body. At that moment, the priest is acting and speaking in Christ's very Person and on His behalf. Acting in Christ's Person

[8]   David Foster Wallace, "This is Water," Farnam Street Media, https://fs.blog/david-foster-wallace-this-is-water/.

includes being male because the priest personifies Christ in the Mass in a very real and intimate way. Christ's maleness is not incidental but essential to His identity. Therefore, only a man has the capacity to act in Christ's Person.

The second reason is related to the first: the Church, following St. Paul's description, is the Bride of Christ; Christ gives His life for the Church, who receives Him as a bride receives her husband. This image is best exemplified during the celebration of the Mass, when, again, the priest acts in Christ's Person. By his ordination, the priest is configured to Christ so that he may imitate Him in sacrificing himself for others.

Third, when Christ chose His apostles, whom He ordained at the Last Supper as the first priests, He chose men only. In perpetuating the priesthood that Christ began, the Church imitates Christ in choosing men only. The Church has no authority to admit women to the priesthood because doing so would contradict the practice of Christ.

It is not the case that Christ's choice of men as His apostles was conditioned by the societal expectations of His time. Christ was constantly transgressing societal expectations in His interactions with men and with women. The choice of men as apostles, then, reflects God's will — not society's preferences.

It is unfortunate that the discussion about reserving the priesthood for men only is shaped by contemporary notions of equality as demonstrated through power. The priesthood is not about power but about configuring a man to Jesus Christ so that he, in imitation of Christ, can lay down his life for the people he serves. But beyond this, the greatest in the kingdom of God are not the ones with the most power or authority but the ones who are most faithful to God. Hence the greatest saint, over and above even the apostles, is the

Blessed Virgin Mary, who had no power nor office and saw herself as nothing more than "the handmaid of the Lord" (Luke 1:38).

73. WHY CAN'T PRIESTS MARRY?

As mentioned in the prior question, the priest is configured to Christ at his ordination. Figuratively speaking, just as Christ is the groom and the Church is His Bride, so the priest marries the Church through his ordination. In imitation of Christ, who lived a celibate life in service of His people, so too does the priest embrace celibacy in order to serve his people with his whole being.

In the history of the Church, there have been married priests. Yet the Church has always prized celibacy as the greatest way for the priest to live his vocation of service. In sacrificing the good of family life, the priest follows Christ into a unique form of love: laying down his life so that others may have life more abundantly.

74. WHY DO CATHOLICS GO TO CONFESSION?

The Sacrament of Penance, also called the Sacrament of Confession or Reconciliation, is a tremendous gift of Christ to His people. Through it, God forgives all our sins and restores our relationship with Him. In this sacrament, we express our contrition, that is, our sorrow for acting contrary to God's love and God's commandments, by confessing our sins to a priest in private.

Admitting our sins aloud to a priest forces us to confront our faults directly to promote both accountability and healing. In the confessional, the priest is the channel for God's forgiveness; the grace of Christ's sacrifice on the Cross touches us directly through the words of the priest. When the priest says the words of absolution from sin, we know for certain that our sins have been forgiven.

It is good and proper to apologize to God for our sins in our private prayer every night before going to sleep. Yet here our contrition does not necessarily receive a direct response from God. When we confess our sins to a priest, we receive God's response immediately, and we leave Confession rejoicing confidently in the mercy that God has sent us through His priest.

The Church encourages us to confess our sins, be they great or small, regularly, or at a minimum of once a year (CCC 1457), so that our souls can be washed in the saving blood of Christ, which helps us grow in love for Him. The Church adds that all mortal sins, that is, grave violations of the Ten Commandments done willingly and with full knowledge of the wrong, must be confessed to a priest in order to be reconciled with God and in order to receive Holy Communion at Mass.

75. IF SOMEONE CONFESSES A CRIME, DOES THE PRIEST NOTIFY THE POLICE?

No. The priest is bound by what is called the "seal of Confession." He may never reveal who has confessed to him or what has been confessed under any circumstances. The Church regards the seal of Confession with the utmost seriousness. In fact, there have been priests who have been martyred for refusing to violate the seal of Confession, such as St. John Nepomucene (1345–1393), whom King Wenceslaus IV of Bohemia ordered drowned when he refused the king's command to disclose what his wife the queen had said in Confession. Catholics, therefore, have complete confidence that what they say to a priest in the confessional stays in the confessional.

CHAPTER 11

CALLING TO GOD IN PRAYER

✝

76. *WHAT IS THE POINT OF PRAYING?*

Prayer is conversation with God. It is the primary way in which we relate to Him, and relationship with God, in this life and in the next, is the goal of our human existence. The more we pray, the more deeply we grow in this relationship. Every time we pray, we have a foretaste of Heaven, where we will spend all eternity in direct communion with God.

When Jesus' disciples asked Him how to pray, He responded with what we call the Lord's Prayer (the Our Father), which encapsulates the spiritual life. God, the Creator of the universe, is worthy of all praise by virtue of His infinite majesty. But He is not just an abstract being; He is the Father of each person who has ever lived, and therefore wants a personal relationship with each one. When His will triumphs on earth, human beings find their joy. Since He is our Father, we rely on Him for all our needs. We ask Him to forgive us our sins and keep us from harm. In the Our Father we find the four elements of prayer: praise, thanksgiving, contrition, and petition.

There are two general ways to pray, and each is essential to the spiritual life. The first is the set prayers of the Church: the Our Father, Hail Mary, Glory Be, the Rosary, the Mass, grace before meals, prayers for the dead, and many others. These help shape our relationship with God by providing the pillars on which faith is based.

The second way is through personal prayer in which we express to God in our own words what is on our minds and in our hearts. Through these two types of prayer, we draw closer to God, who rejoices each time we call upon Him.

77. *HOW DO I KNOW GOD IS LISTENING?*

As our Father, God is always attentive to our every need when we speak to Him. Jesus assures each of us of our infinite value before God: "Even the hairs of your head are all numbered" (Matt. 10:30).

He also emphasized God's attentiveness to our prayers: "When you pray, go into your room and shut the door and pray to your Father who is in secret; and your Father who sees in secret will reward you" (Matt. 6:6); "What man of you, if his son asks him for bread, will give him a stone? Or if he asks for a fish, will give him a serpent? If you then, who are evil, know how to give good gifts to your children, how much more will your Father who is in heaven give good things to those who ask him!" (Matt. 7:9–11); "Will not God vindicate his elect, who cry to him day and night? Will he delay long over them?" (Luke 18:7); "Truly, truly, I say to you, if you ask anything of the Father, He will give it to you in my name.... Ask, and you will receive, that your joy may be full" (John 16:23–24).

God is not a vindictive miser sitting in the sky looking to punish malefactors. He is love and He created us to share His love with us. Our prayers delight Him because whenever we pray, we reach out to receive and to return His love.

78. *MY PRAYERS ARE NOT ALWAYS ANSWERED –*
AM I PRAYING THE RIGHT WAY?

Jesus told us, "Ask, and it will be given you; seek, and you will find; knock, and it will be opened to you" (Matt. 7:7). Yet sometimes it seems our prayers go unanswered. We pray for the recovery of a loved one, yet he dies. Or we pray to receive a new job, but it goes to someone else.

How do we know, then, if we are praying the right way? Prayer is simply a conversation with God, but it can be weighed down by our worldly concerns, fears, and anxieties. Other times our sins make us feel far away from God, or we become angry with God because we are grieving, or we are simply experiencing a time of dryness when God feels absent. For all these reasons, we cannot trust our feelings alone to determine the right way to pray.

Difficulties in prayer are a normal part of the spiritual experience. Think of the prayer of Jesus in the Garden of Gethsemane at the most intense moment of His life: "Abba, Father, all things are possible to thee; remove this cup from me; yet not what I will, but what thou wilt" (Mark 14:36).

From Jesus' agony in the Garden, we learn two things. First, to be granted, our petition must conform with God's will, which is directed not necessarily toward our perceived present needs within the world but toward our own eternal salvation. What may seem essential to us in the moment may not be essential to arriving in Heaven at some future moment, which is God's chief concern. In acknowledging the priority of the Father's will in His own prayer, Jesus teaches us that only God can see the full picture of salvation. Second, when we petition God, we are placing our trust in His divine omnipotence. When our petitions do not turn out as we desired, we must make the more difficult act of trusting His divine omniscience. He knows what we need.

In times of spiritual challenge, we should remember the advice of St. Paul: "Rejoice always, pray constantly, give thanks in all circumstances; for this is the will of God in Christ Jesus for you" (1 Thess. 5:16–18). When we make this act of trust, we become like the little children Jesus spoke of: "Unless you turn and become like children, you will never enter the kingdom of heaven" (Matt. 18:3). Like children petitioning their parents, so must we petition our Father in Heaven, for our salvation requires that we love unconditionally Him who can do all things.

79. IS IT GOD . . . OR A COINCIDENCE?

As noted earlier (Q2), in the eyes of God there are no coincidences. That is, everything that happens in life happens within God's full view and understanding (Q18). God does not will evil nor sin; they are the result of human beings misusing their freedom. Yet from the evil and sin of human beings God continues His plan of uniting all of creation to Himself, who is goodness and love.

In life, then, there are no coincidences. God sends blessings, joys, trials, and sufferings through the most mundane occurrences. The task of the Catholic is to discern God's will in any given situation and try to grow spiritually from the experience.

80. HOW DOES PRAYER WORK?

Jesus instructs us to pray, assuring us that "your Father who sees in secret will reward you" (Matt. 6:6). He gives no hints as to how His Father will reward us, but we can be confident that it will be in ways that we will never expect or imagine. God's workings are infinitely greater than our own.

To help imagine how our prayers work, consider the water cycle. Water evaporates from the earth and is stored in the atmosphere in clouds, which move across the world with the weather. Eventually, certain clouds become full and then rain falls, perhaps thousands of miles from where the droplets first coalesced.

Our prayers work in an analogous fashion: we send our prayers up to God, who receives them and then eventually, according to His time and not ours, sends His grace down to the earth as an answer to our prayers. Our prayers may help those who live thousands of miles away, in different time periods, or even outside of time, as is the case for prayers offered for souls in Purgatory.

When we die and go before God in judgment for an accounting of our lives, we will see all the ways our prayers have inspired answers through God's generosity. Every time we pray, our relationship with God deepens. Ours is a relationship of trust, so, in praying, we trust that God will put our prayers to good use on His terms rather than on ours.

81. WHAT IS A EUCHARISTIC MIRACLE?

In the Eucharist, Jesus is present to us in a very special way. The host that we see, though it looks like ordinary bread, is no longer bread after it is consecrated by a priest during the Mass. It is Jesus Christ Himself, truly present in His Body, Blood, soul, and divinity, though hidden from our sight. Only faith can see Jesus in the Eucharist, and we believe He is there because He told us so: "Take this, all of you, and eat of it. This is my Body which is given up for you" (see Mark 14:22).

Yet in the course of time, Christ has occasionally bolstered our faith by revealing His presence in the Eucharist before our eyes. The first scientifically verified eucharistic miracle occurred in the eighth century in a village called Lanciano in Italy. Since then, more than one hundred eucharistic miracles verified by Church authorities have occurred throughout the world.

In recent years, eucharistic miracles have occurred in Chirattakonam, India (2001); Tixtla, Mexico (2006); Sokolka, Poland (2008); and Legnica, Poland (2013). All of them have been examined by scientists using the latest laboratory equipment, which found the same traits present in all the tested host-flesh tissue: it is human cardiac tissue with human blood, type AB, the same blood that is found on the Shroud of Turin, the burial cloth of Jesus. The miracles have also been examined by Church authorities who have approved them for veneration by the faithful. In these cases, science has confirmed our Faith as reasonable.

Books and websites that showcase the eucharistic miracles are readily available. These miracles are gifts from God by which He transcends the natural order to help us believe in Him more deeply.

82. WHY DO CATHOLICS PRAY TO MARY AND THE SAINTS?

Catholics do not travel through life alone. Nor do we relate to God on our own. In fact, we cannot come to faith without the help of others who lead us to Baptism and teach us what to believe and how to live. Baptism makes us brothers and sisters in Christ; as fellow members of God's family we each have an obligation to help our fellow believers in any way possible, and praying for one another is a chief way we help. Naturally, then, when we are in need, we can and should ask our family and friends to pray for us. The more people beseeching God's grace on our behalf, the better.

In this spirit, Catholics pray to Mary and the saints to enlist their assistance with our needs. It is a great gift when our friends pray for us; it is a greater gift when Mary and the saints, who are also our brothers and sisters in Baptism and who are now so close to God, pray for us. In worldly things, we hear the expression, "I will take all the help I can get." The same goes for spiritual things: we want all the help we can get. Mary and the saints, by virtue of our union with them, can be our greatest aids as we reach up to God, not as isolated individuals, but as members of a family who inhabit Heaven and earth.

CHAPTER 12

HEAVEN – AND WHO GOES THERE

†

83. WHY SHOULD I CARE ABOUT THE NEXT LIFE WHEN THERE ARE SO MANY THINGS TO THINK ABOUT IN THIS ONE?

First, the good things in this life are gifts from God, and they point us back to Him insofar as they are good. These goods rightly please us, yet they cannot completely satisfy our relentless drive for good and for love. In this way, the good things in life foreshadow the infinite good that is God, whom we will see directly in Heaven.

Second, in a real way, life after death is not radically distinct from our lives here on earth. Eternal life with God is the fulfillment of our earthly lives. It begins not at death, but when we are baptized, at which moment God adopts us as His sons and daughters for all eternity. We then spend our earthly lives living and developing that filial relationship.

The life we find after death — eternal happiness with God or eternal punishment in Hell — is the culmination of the lives we led on earth. If we lived well with God on earth, we will continue to live well with Him in Heaven; only the nature of our relationship changes. Likewise, if we ignored God in this life, using the goods of the earth to gratify only ourselves, then we will continue to live without God after death in Hell.

84. MY PROTESTANT FRIEND ASKS IF I'M SAVED. WHAT SHOULD I SAY?

Martin Luther rejected the Church's understanding of salvation as a gift won by Christ's death that we must actively receive and then live out each day of our lives. Luther fashioned his own understanding of salvation whereby a person is saved the moment he accepts Christ as his Savior in Baptism. Over time, different Protestant groups, particularly some Calvinists, taught "once saved, always saved." In other words, once a person has accepted Christ, his salvation can never be lost no matter what sin he commits. And yet Scripture teaches us that salvation is not a one-time event, but a process that begins with Baptism and then is worked out over a lifetime of living in union with God and His Church. We call this process "growing in holiness."

Becoming holy is typically not a straight linear progression upward: we step forward, then fall back when we sin, then begin to climb again when we confess our sins. At any point, a person can reject God's love and mercy, even if he was once faithful. Should he make this fatal choice, he would not be saved, for he would be rejecting Christ's gift of salvation.

St. Paul instructed the Philippians to "work out your own salvation with fear and trembling; for God is at work in you, both to will and to work for his good pleasure" (Phil. 2:12–13). Since applying the salvation Christ freely offers to us is a perpetual work in progress, Catholics are right, in humility and in awareness of God's majesty, to say that they do not know for certain whether they will be saved, but that they hope in God's mercy that they will be.

85. *ARE HEAVEN AND HELL REAL PLACES?*

Based on Jesus' repeated statements, we are certain that Heaven and Hell are real places, although not geographical places we can find on a map. Heaven is with God, who transcends the limits of time and space. Aside from Jesus' general descriptions, we know precious little about it. Heaven has often been described as living the "Beatific Vision," meaning that we live the unbridled joy of seeing God face to face for all eternity. Pope Benedict XVI, in his encyclical *Spe Salvi*, beautifully described Heaven as

> the supreme moment of satisfaction, in which totality embraces us and we embrace totality.... It would be like plunging into the ocean of infinite love, a moment in which time — the before and after — no longer exists. We can only attempt to grasp the idea that such a moment is life in the full sense, a plunging ever anew into the vastness of being, in which we are simply overwhelmed with joy. This is how Jesus expresses it in Saint John's Gospel: "I will see you again and your hearts will rejoice, and no one will take your joy from you."[9]

Hell, by contrast, is permanent absence from God. In Hell we are completely enfolded in our own ego, which pushes God away. God is love; He, therefore, is not wanted there. As the nameless pastor in George Bernanos's novel *Diary of a Country Priest* puts it, "Hell is not to love anymore."

What exactly Hell is like has been the subject of artistic imagination for two millennia. It may be a place of fiery torment or it may be

---

[9]   Benedict XVI, Encyclical Letter on Christian Hope *Spe Salvi* (November 30, 2007), no. 12.

colder than ice, as Dante envisioned its innermost recesses. However it is, it is a place of punishment, sadness, and anger, for the lost soul is aware that he is separated from God for all eternity. Where God is excluded, there can be neither joy nor love.

86. WHAT HAPPENS TO THOSE WHO NEVER HEAR ABOUT JESUS – WILL THEY GO TO HEAVEN?

Jesus Christ makes belief in Him an essential element of salvation. For example, consider His response to the apostle Thomas at the Last Supper: "I am the way, and the truth, and the life; no one comes to the Father, but by me" (John 14:6). But belief is a free choice for each person, so it is fair to wonder what happens to those who, not having heard of Jesus, cannot make that choice.

Concerning these questions, the Second Vatican Council's *Lumen Gentium* teaches,

> Those also can attain to salvation who through no fault of their own do not know the Gospel of Christ or His Church, yet sincerely seek God and moved by grace strive by their deeds to do His will as it is known to them through the dictates of conscience. Nor does Divine Providence deny the helps necessary for salvation to those who, without blame on their part, have not yet arrived at an explicit knowledge of God and with His grace strive to live a good life. Whatever good or truth is found amongst them is looked upon by the Church as a preparation for the Gospel.[10]

---

[10] Vatican Council II, Dogmatic Constitution on the Church *Lumen Gentium* (November 21, 1964), no. 16.

First, the Council's emphasis on personal responsibility — "through no fault of their own," "without blame on their part" — is important: a person has to be completely unaware of God, of Christ, and of the Catholic Church to count as "never exposed."

Second, the Council is circumspect in its language: God will aid those who have never heard of Him or of Christ so they have a chance at salvation. The Council does not teach that they *will* be saved. All who are saved, the Council teaches, are saved through Christ crucified, whether they are aware of Him or not. The good works that these people do point them in the direction of God, who is the author of all that is good. God can extend His mercy to these people as He does to those who believe in Him.

It is unfashionable to remark on this fact, but it is undeniable: although God desires all persons to be saved, He makes it easier for some to be saved than others. This may strike us as unfair, but God works the same way in the natural order: some have more advantages in life — intelligence, strength, looks, and wealth — than others. For a few, life can be a slog from birth to death. Yet somehow, in ways known to God and not to us, each human life is equally precious to Him.

The same goes for salvation: God makes it easier for some than others, yet He still has a plan whereby all His creatures can share in eternity with Him. Catholics have the greatest opportunity for salvation; Christians have greater opportunities than those of other monotheistic religions; these, in turn, have greater opportunities than pagans, who have greater opportunities than nonbelievers.

It follows that to be a baptized Catholic is to receive the greatest gift possible on the road to salvation because the Catholic Church possesses all that we need to get there: God's commandments, Christ Himself, the Bible, the sacraments, the Church as Christ's Body led by the pope and bishops, and the Church's teachings.

The inverse of this is also true: to reject the gift that is the Catholic Church jeopardizes a person's opportunity for salvation. As *Lumen Gentium* chillingly states, "Whosoever, therefore, knowing that the Catholic Church was made necessary by Christ, would refuse to enter or to remain in it, could not be saved."[11]

Salvation is a gift of God that none of us earns or deserves. Our free response to this gift is necessary. To live the Catholic Faith to the full is the most effective way to receive God's salvation. It follows that to be Catholic is a tremendous gift that we must receive with an open heart.

87. CAN FOLLOWERS OF OTHER RELIGIONS GO TO HEAVEN?

According to the Second Vatican Council's *Lumen Gentium*, it is possible for adherents of other religions to go to Heaven if they were unaware of the necessity of the Catholic Church for salvation and if they lived according to the moral law. However, it is critical to add that followers of other religions who do reach Heaven do *not* do so because of their religion. They are saved by Christ Himself through the mercy of God whose grace extends to them through the Catholic Church, which is the storehouse of His grace.

Jesus Christ is the only means of salvation, and the Catholic Church, joined to Christ, perpetuates His salvation in time. Yet God can save anyone whom He wishes who is outside the Church. As *Lumen Gentium* makes clear, all human beings should seek the Catholic Church, where they find all the means to facilitate their journeys to God.

---

[11] Ibid., no. 14.

88. *CAN A PERSON NOT BELIEVE IN GOD BUT STILL BE SAVED?*

All human beings can perform good works, regardless of their beliefs, and all human beings are capable of loving others out of a variety of motives, even if they do not believe in God.

Personal responsibility matters. A person who unwittingly does not believe in God and does good works can be saved. But a person who wrestles with whether God exists and then chooses not to believe in Him likely cannot be saved. This is a logical consequence of the nonbeliever's choice: If a person completely rejects God in this life, how can God accept Him in the next life? God does not force us to accept His salvation. If a person chooses not to believe in Him, he also chooses not to be saved by Him.

89. *IF A CATHOLIC FALLS AWAY FROM THE CHURCH, DOES GOD STILL ACCEPT THAT PERSON?*

The Second Vatican Council's *Lumen Gentium* issues a sobering warning to Catholics who fail to live up to the gift they have received in being baptized into the Church:

> All the Church's children should remember that their exalted status is to be attributed not to their own merits but to the special grace of Christ. If they fail moreover to respond to that grace in thought, word

and deed, not only shall they not be saved but they
will be the more severely judged.[12]

To fall away from the Church is a terrible sin whereby Catholics reject
the special grace of Christ. It is true that several factors outside of a
person's control may contribute to his falling away and thus diminish
his guilt: poor instruction in the Faith, having one or both parents
who do not practice the Faith, the pervasive influence of a culture
hostile to religion, poor or even horrific treatment by clergy or by
other Catholics.

Yet the choice to leave — whether it happens gradually or at
once — belongs to the individual, and it is the person who is ulti-
mately responsible for choosing a path contrary to God's given path.
The Council does not mince words: those who knowingly reject the
Church reject God, and, as a result, they likely will not be saved by
God.

---

[12] Ibid.

CHAPTER 13

WHAT HAPPENS WHEN WE DIE

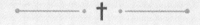

WHAT HAPPENS WHEN WE DIE

✝

90. *HOW DO WE KNOW THERE IS LIFE AFTER DEATH?*

We have a sense that there is life after death in the natural order because of the reality of the soul. The soul (Q14), the animating principle of the body that makes each of us who we are, is immaterial, meaning that it is not made of physical substance, and therefore it is not subject to death and decay. If the soul cannot die, it must live on after the person dies.

The ancient Greek philosophers realized this without the aid of revelation and crafted myths to account for the continued life of the soul after death, as the nature of this hidden life exceeds the powers of human reason.

Beyond this, what we know about life after death comes from God's revelation to us in Jesus Christ, who promised at the Last Supper that "[i]n my Father's house are many rooms; if it were not so, would I have told you that I go to prepare a place for you?" (John 14:2). When the "good thief" crucified on Good Friday asked Jesus to remember him when Jesus entered into His kingdom, He replied, "Truly, I say to you, today you will be with me in Paradise" (Luke 23:43).

Throughout His public ministry, Jesus spoke of judgment after death, of eternal life in Heaven, and of punishment in Hell, which He referred to as *Sheol*. He taught about judgment, Heaven, and Hell so often, both directly and in parable form, that we can be certain that these are realities that await us after death.

91. *WHAT HAPPENS AFTER WE DIE?*

Death is the greatest mystery human beings encounter, and before the coming of Christ it was downright terrifying — there was no definitive hope of life beyond the grave. Christ's Resurrection lifts that fear. Now, though we naturally are anxious about death because we leave everyone behind and because its specifics are unknown, with faith we know that Christ, our brother, awaits us on the other side.

At the moment of death, the soul separates from the body and goes before God, who will judge us according to how well — or poorly — we lived our lives. We call this the *Particular Judgment*. A life well lived is spent in service of God and of others, as Jesus commanded; this service includes keeping God's commandments. As judge, God is both perfectly just and perfectly merciful — a paradox for us but not for God. For sure, our sins are evil and deserve punishment, yet the same God who judges us also died in our place to pay the debt for our sins, and He did this because He loves us. So we approach God our judge with fear and joy, with worry and hope, with dread and anticipation.

From there we are destined for eternal life with God or eternal separation from Him; the former is Heaven and the latter Hell. Souls found worthy of Heaven must first be cleansed of all stain of sin that was present at the moment of death, for sin is incompatible with the perfection that is God; we call this cleansing *Purgatory*. Only then will souls be prepared to stand before the incomprehensible awesomeness of God in Heaven.

When God decides to bring the world to an end, then a second judgment, called the *Final Judgment,* will occur. The souls of every person who ever lived will be called before God the judge in a manner similar to Jesus' warning:

> When the Son of man comes in his glory, and all the angels with him, then he will sit on his glorious throne. Before him will be gathered all the nations, and he will separate them one from another as a shepherd separates the sheep from the goats, and he will place the sheep at his right hand, but the goats at the left (Matt. 25:31–33).

The righteous souls on His right will remain in God's loving presence forever while the wicked souls will be irreversibly condemned to Hell.

92. ARE WE ALL PREDESTINED FOR HEAVEN OR HELL?

God knows everything that each of us has done and will do, and thus knows whether we will go to Heaven or Hell at the end of our lives. But He knows that not because He predestined us, in the sense of sending us to either place without our willing it. Rather, God knows what we will do because all time — past, present, future — equally appear before Him in His divine mind (Q5).

God does not coerce any of our actions. The famous parable of the prodigal son (Luke 15:11–32) shows just how much God respects our freedom: He even allows us to insult and reject Him. Moreover, we have the example of Judas and the other actors who orchestrated Christ's execution: God did not intervene to stop them, nor did He force them to act as they did. The same goes for our own lives: we feel no compulsion by God to act for good or for evil, which means we, without our own consent, cannot be predestined by God to Heaven or Hell.

93. WHY DOES THE CHURCH OPPOSE ASSISTED SUICIDE (EUTHANASIA)?

We have already said that God is the author of life, who grants this gift as He wills, in ways that we will never understand. As such, even though each person has the power to live as he pleases, the ultimate authority of life and death does not belong to him. God decides when we are born and when we will die. Death is part of nature in our fallen world. Hence human beings must respect the process of death and allow it to happen as it will.

Assisted suicide, also called *euthanasia*, takes the life of a person who is sick or dying. It is wrong and a sin because it is murder concealed under the false guise of compassion. It rejects God as the ultimate authority over life and death.

Today it is often argued that those who are suffering terribly from terminal illness have a poor "quality of life" due to pain and the certain proximity of death, so they should be allowed to end their lives with the help of medicine. This "quality of life" argument is repulsively utilitarian as it instrumentalizes human life to what a human being can produce and endure. It rejects the fact that life is sacred and has an intrinsic value regardless of how great a person's sufferings are. This value comes from God, who willed the person into existence and will take that person back to Him whenever He sees that the time is right. As Pope St. John Paul II wrote in his encyclical *Evangelium Vitae*, "Man is called to a fullness of life which far exceeds the dimensions of his earthly existence, because it consists in sharing the very life of God."[13]

94. HOW CAN I HELP SOMEONE WHO IS DYING – OR HAS DIED?

The best thing to do for someone who is dying is to call a priest, who will help the person prepare to meet God in the best spiritual shape possible through administration of the sacraments. Calling a priest is the special responsibility of adult children who are caring for their dying parents. Ideally, the Sacrament of the Anointing of the Sick, whose purpose is to strengthen the soul in its final agony, includes a final confession of sins and a final reception of Holy Communion, called *Viaticum*, which means "food for the journey." Hence a priest should be called when the dying person is still conscious, if that is possible. Anointing of the Sick still benefits someone who has lost consciousness, but Confession and Holy Communion cannot be made.

The prayer that accompanies the anointing reveals this sacrament as a beautiful gift of God to His children in their final battle: "Through this holy anointing may the Lord in his love and mercy help you with the grace of the Holy Spirit. May the Lord who frees you from sin save you and raise you up."

It is necessary to pray for the dead always, but the greatest prayer for someone who has died is to arrange for a Mass to be offered for the repose of his soul. During the sacrifice of the Mass, the infinite merits of Christ's saving sacrifice on the Cross atone for the sins of

[13] John Paul II, Encyclical Letter on the Value and Inviolability of Human Life *Evangelium Vitae* (March 25, 1995), no. 2.

the deceased. Souls can leave Purgatory and enter Heaven through the power of the Mass, through which all those in Heaven "have washed their robes and made them white in the blood of the Lamb" (Rev. 7:14).

CHAPTER 14

GETTING BACK ON TRACK WITH GOD

†

95. *IF I SKIP MASS ONE WEEK, CAN I RECEIVE EUCHARIST THE NEXT WEEK?*

No. We have already said that to receive Holy Communion is to come into union with Christ Himself, the deepest union possible this side of eternity (Q69). If a person intentionally misses Mass, he is telling Christ that he is not interested in union with Him, that he has other things he values above Him.

To miss Mass intentionally, therefore, is a very grave sin that breaks a person's relationship with Christ. So, before the person can enter into union with Christ again in Holy Communion, he has to have that union repaired first by going to the Sacrament of Penance to confess his sin. Holy Communion does not create union between Christ and the recipient out of thin air; it consummates a union that already exists as a pledge of deeper love. Once the union is reconciled, the gift that is Holy Communion can be received again with joy and gratitude.

Each time we receive Christ, the Son of God, in the Eucharist, we are drawn up into the inner life of the Holy Trinity — Father, Son, and Holy Spirit — whom we will see face to face after death. We can have this awesome experience each time we attend Mass. Knowing this, we should not only never miss Mass on Sunday, but we should eagerly desire to attend each week to enter into union with the Trinity.

96. CAN A PERSON HAVE A STRONG RELATIONSHIP WITH GOD, EVEN WHEN NOT FULLY BELIEVING ALL TEACHINGS OF THE CHURCH?

To believe the Church's teachings is to believe God. So, first, it does not make sense to accept some of the Church's teachings while rejecting others. Since they come from the same source, they have the same validity. To use an image, if one branch of a tree should be diseased, the entire tree would be infected. But since the tree that is the Church grows from divine soil, it cannot be diseased. All of her teachings are true because they all come from God (Q66).

Second, while someone can have a decent relationship with God without believing all the teachings of the Church, his relationship will never be complete because there will always be a "sticking point" between him and God. Since God created us for relationship, He is grieved whenever His children create an obstacle that prevents Him from enveloping them with His divine love. The key to any relationship, including our relationship with God, hinges on the mutual trust between persons. When someone does not believe or accept a teaching of the Church, he does not trust God who entrusted that teaching to the Church.

In our world today it is not surprising that some Catholics may have difficulty understanding or believing Church teaching. The proper response of Catholics in this situation is to pray for the grace to overcome their fears and embrace all the teachings in faith, knowing that doing so will allow them to embrace God more confidently.

97. WHAT SHOULD I DO IF SOMEONE I LOVE HAS WALKED AWAY FROM THE CHURCH?

The first and most important thing to do is to pray for that person. Ask God to send the Holy Spirit to soften his heart so he will open himself to receive God's love again. Pray that, like the prodigal son, this person will come to his senses and return to his loving Father, who with tender mercy will take the lost soul back as soon as he confesses his sins and asks for forgiveness.

In addition, try to understand both the stated reason for the person's decision to leave and any hidden motivations that may exist. Find an opportunity to engage the person in a calm and friendly manner. Ask the person to articulate his reasons for leaving and then try to address them one at a time without condemning him. It is always difficult for a person to admit wrongdoing or wrong thinking in any matter; religious issues can be even more difficult to acknowledge because they touch a person's inner core.

Lastly, realize that an initial conversation is not likely to tip the scales. The person has to remove the obstacles to God that he has erected in his own soul before he can feel God's love again. That may take an insufferably long time, which is why we must continue to persevere in prayer for that person and keep the lines of communication with him open to help him continue his journey back to God and His Church.

98. WHAT SHOULD I DO IF I HAVE LEFT THE CHURCH AND NOW WANT TO RETURN?

The Christian story is one of sin and forgiveness. From beginning to end, the Bible tells the stories of so many who sinned, who rejected God, who denied Christ, and who then were received back into God's loving embrace. Moses committed murder. King David committed adultery and orchestrated murder. Peter denied he even knew Jesus three times. Yet these men, once forgiven, received special tasks from God to serve as human pillars from which the Church extends. Truly, no one is outside of God's mercy — not even you.

The first step in returning to the Church is to follow the examples of Moses, King David, and Peter: to acknowledge your sins and confess them, including that of leaving the Church for however long, to a priest in the Sacrament of Penance. This will reconcile you with God, fill you with grace, and renew you both spiritually and mentally.

Once forgiven, you can then resume your Catholic life by attending Mass each week, receiving Holy Communion, and praying daily to strengthen your relationship with God. There is more that can be done — learning more about the Faith, partaking in acts of charity — but Mass and prayer are the foundational actions of Catholics trying to work out their salvation.

The prodigal son (Q66, 92, 97) is the model for those who have fallen away and wish to return to the Church. Once you, like him, acknowledge your sins and confess them, you will find a loving and generous Father ready to return you to His family and embrace you with love.

99. HOW CAN I KEEP MY FAITH IF I HAVE DOUBTS?

Trusting in God despite the challenges, fears, and sufferings we face is how we show our love for Him. Even in the midst of the storms of our lives, we can reassure ourselves of God's ultimate control over everything by reading the Bible, where story after story shows Him as the one with the power. To cite one famous example, consider how Jesus rescued the disciples when their boat was caught in a storm:

> And a great storm of wind arose, and the waves beat into the boat, so that the boat was already filling. But he was in the stern, asleep on the cushion; and they woke him and said to him, "Teacher, do you not care if we

perish?" And he awoke and rebuked the wind, and said
to the sea, "Peace! Be still!" And the wind ceased, and
there was a great calm. He said to them, "Why are you
afraid? Have you no faith?" And they were filled with
awe, and said to one another, "Who then is this, that
even wind and sea obey him?" (Mark 4:37–41)

How can we trust God when we are in the middle of a stormy
time, when our own doubts assail us and tempt us to turn from God?

Catholics often experience feelings of uneasiness when they encounter aspects of their Faith they do not readily understand. And
yet God in His mercy will help us to overcome these feelings of unease, if we ask for help.

First, and most importantly, pray to God for enlightenment to see
what God intends in the situation or in the teaching of the Church. Ask
for more grace to trust God and to deepen your faith in Him.

Second, speak with a priest or spiritual director to help clarify
any difficulties or uneasy feelings about God or His Church and
work for resolutions with their guidance.

Third, if the unease comes from a Church teaching, read more
deeply into it, seeking commentary on it or clarifications from
knowledgeable sources. The *Catechism of the Catholic Church*, which
summarizes all of Catholic teaching, is a perfect place to begin before
digging deeper.

Fourth, with any difficult situation, the writings of the saints can
inspire faith and provide practical solutions for difficulties. St. Teresa
of Ávila's *Interior Castle* will guide those having difficulties in prayer; St.
John Henry Newman's *Apologia Pro Vita Sua* and *Essay Concerning the
Development of Christian Doctrine* brilliantly explain the role of the
Church as teacher and how Church teachings emanate from Christ.

100. *HOW CAN I BUILD UP MY SPIRITUAL LIFE?*

Building up the soul by engaging in the spiritual life is analogous to building up the body, which requires regular exercise, healthy food, rest, and self-discipline to maximize health.

The soul's exercise is prayer (Q76-78). The more time a person spends in prayer, the stronger his soul becomes. As we have already said, prayer is conversation with God; every time a person prays, he comes into union with Him. The healthy food for the soul is the sacraments, which communicate God's divine life to us directly (Q67). Above all, receiving Christ Himself in Holy Communion is the greatest source of grace this side of eternity. The more frequently a person receives Holy Communion — at least weekly, but more often if possible — the stronger his spiritual life will become. An additional source of food is the moral law and the Church's teachings, for they instruct us how to live well.

Next, since rest hints at leisure, the rest for the soul is living Sunday as a day to worship God, to spend quality time with family and friends, and to delve into resources that can deepen our faith, from books to art to podcasts. The more a person comes to know about God, the more he will love Him, and the love of God is the key to a healthy spiritual life. Finally, as self-discipline moderates what the body takes in by avoiding excesses of food, drink, or rest, self-discipline moderates the soul through the practice of fasting, by which the person learns to abstain from temptation, regulate his inclinations toward worldly things, and refocus his energy on God.

CONCLUSION: NOW WHAT?

†

THE ANSWERS TO THE preceding questions are intended as first steps to loving Christ more deeply and trusting His Church that He founded as the means to encounter Him. Consider how Jesus called Matthew, a tax collector and sinner, to follow Him as one of His apostles. Matthew had to overcome a number of obstacles — his own sins, his attachments to his prior lifestyle, his rejection by his fellow Jews — to begin his journey of faith. By trusting Jesus, he did so.

These answers show the reasonableness of faith and of a personal relationship with God in Christ. Yet they are neither exhaustive nor comprehensive. More complete answers to these questions can be found in the *Catechism of the Catholic Church* and in other teachings of the Church, especially as expressed by the writings of Pope St. John Paul II and Pope Benedict XVI.

Once the obstacles to faith are overcome, Catholics can take steps to enter into a deeper relationship with God. First, regular prayer should become a habit. Prayer is our time with God to talk with Him and sit in His presence. It is the air we breathe to fortify our souls.

Second, recourse to the sacraments — weekly Mass, if not more often, and regular confession of sins — brings Catholics into the heart of the Catholic Faith: Christ's Passion, death, and

Resurrection that He undertook to free us from sin and bring us into union with Him forever.

Third, learning how to live the Faith from spiritual masters helps Catholics navigate a turbulent world through time-honored practices. There are two books that stand out as starters: St. Francis de Sales's *Introduction to the Devout Life* and Thomas à Kempis's *Imitation of Christ*. The former book presents a practical guide to every aspect of Catholic living: prayer, overcoming vices, and developing virtues; the latter concentrates on developing the soul in relation to Christ. Both employ chapters that are a few pages in length, so these books can be used in prayer in addition to being read for information.

It is no secret that today's world has rapidly become more secular, which is another word for de-Christianized or post-Christian. In this climate, it is far more difficult for Catholics to know their Faith and live it to the full. By overcoming the obstacles that the post-Christian world has helped to erect, Catholics can walk more easily and more confidently toward Jesus Christ, who is the Way, the Truth, the Life, and the very reason for our existence.

†

ACKNOWLEDGEMENTS

Answering impromptu questions is one of my favorite parts of being a teacher. My mind races, the students are engaged, and learning is maximized in the thrill of the moment. When I heard that the top reason for young people quitting the Catholic Church is that they never had their questions about the faith answered, the idea for this book arose instantly.

I'm grateful to Charlie McKinney and his wonderful team at Sophia Institute Press for believing that these questions and their straightforward answers would make for a compelling book that can help Catholics grow in their faith. Heidi Saxton improved this book with her thoughtful suggestions, concise diction, and clever ideas for reordering questions and chapters. I am indebted to my friend Fr. Joseph Scolaro and to my eldest son Joe for reading drafts of the manuscript and offering excellent suggestions to improve my answers. Any errors that remain are my own.

Above all, I'm grateful to those, especially my own students, who anonymously asked sincere questions that showed they were seeking the Lord and requesting help in their search. It is my prayer that the answers in this book help them find Him.

†

ABOUT THE AUTHOR

DAVID G. BONAGURA JR. is an adjunct professor at St. Joseph's Seminary and Catholic International University and a teacher at Regis High School. He is the author of *Steadfast in Faith* and *Staying with the Catholic Church* and the translator of *Jerome's Tears: Letters to Friends in Mourning.*

Sophia Institute

SOPHIA INSTITUTE IS A nonprofit institution that seeks to nurture the spiritual, moral, and cultural life of souls and to spread the gospel of Christ in conformity with the authentic teachings of the Roman Catholic Church.

Sophia Institute Press fulfills this mission by offering translations, reprints, and new publications that afford readers a rich source of the enduring wisdom of mankind.

Sophia Institute also operates the popular online resource CatholicExchange.com. *Catholic Exchange* provides world news from a Catholic perspective as well as daily devotionals and articles that will help readers to grow in holiness and live a life consistent with the teachings of the Church.

In 2013, Sophia Institute launched Sophia Institute for Teachers to renew and rebuild Catholic culture through service to Catholic education. With the goal of nurturing the spiritual, moral, and cultural life of souls, and an abiding respect for the role and work of teachers, we strive to provide materials and programs that are at once enlightening to the mind and ennobling to the heart; faithful and complete, as well as useful and practical.

Sophia Institute gratefully recognizes the Solidarity Association for preserving and encouraging the growth of our apostolate over the course of many years. Without their generous and timely support, this book would not be in your hands.

www.SophiaInstitute.com
www.CatholicExchange.com
www.SophiaTeachers.org

Sophia Institute Press is a registered trademark of Sophia Institute.
Sophia Institute is a tax-exempt institution as defined by the
Internal Revenue Code, Section 501(c)(3). Tax ID 22-2548708.